EXALT HIM!

EXALT HIM!

Designing Dynamic Worship Services

TERRY WARDLE

CHRISTIAN PUBLICATIONS
CAMP HILL, PENNSYLVANIA

*To my loving wife
and best friend, Cheryl,
and to our three precious children,
Aaron, Cara and Emily.*

Christian Publications
3825 Hartzdale Drive, Camp Hill PA 17011

The mark of ✝ *vibrant faith*

ISBN: 0-87509-413-9
LOC Catalog Card Number: 88-72024
© 1988, 1992 by Christian Publications
All rights reserved
Printed in the United States of America

95 4 3 2

CONTENTS

FOREWORD

Too MANY CHURCHES in the United States and Canada are in the worship doldrums. The most important weekly event in the life of the church turns out to be a loser—dull, predictable, uninspiring.

Faithful church members endure the routine week after week without giving it much thought. After all, most of them have little to compare it with. For the privilege of eternal salvation through Jesus Christ, they will pay almost any price, including boring Sunday worship services.

From time to time, they wonder why their church has not grown. But in their speculation they rarely include the quality of their worship service.

Pastors in general take worship for granted. They do it the way it has always been done. Worship is filling up an hour with two or three prayers, two or three congregational songs, a choir anthem, a sermon, some announcements and an offering. Putting a Sunday service together is one of the easiest of the pastor's duties, because, except for the sermon, little or no creativity is required. It is automatic. And many of these pastors wonder why their churches do not grow.

Terry Wardle says it does not have to be this way. In this book he tells us that stodgy worship patterns can be changed and that worship services, whether in large or in small churches, can be exciting. I have known Terry for years and have admired him as a specialist in church growth who knows how to communicate growth principles in a forceful and practical way. With this book, my admiration has soared, because in it he has pioneered efforts to show systematically how worship relates to church growth.

Over the past decade or so, a new awareness of the centrality of worship in church life has appeared across the board. Creative research and teaching is proliferating, and Terry is in close touch with what is going on in the field. One of the outstanding features of this book is that Terry's stimulating ideas have been reinforced by what God is showing to many other experts in the field of worship.

If you want the worship life of your church to glorify God, to center on Jesus Christ, to edify believers and to appeal to those who visit your church, this book will help you make it do these things. If worship as uplifting and inspiring celebration sounds good to you, read on. If your congregation would like to become participants rather than just remain as spectators in lifting Jesus higher on Sunday morning, *Exalt Him! Designing Dynamic Worship Services* is for you.

Try it and perhaps questions as to why your church is not growing will no longer have to be asked.

C. Peter Wagner
Fuller Theological Seminary
Pasadena, California

A SMALL BOY SAT beside his mother in church. Like most children, his attention was neither easily captured nor readily held. So much of what was happening in the service seemed uninteresting, unrelated, unimportant. Quite frankly, he was bored stiff! Suddenly his ever-wandering eyes noticed a bronze plaque prominently placed upon the side wall. There he saw stars, letters and the outline of an American flag. Nudging his mother and pointing to the plaque, he asked, "What's that?" Graciously and patiently the young mother replied, "Oh, those are the names of people from our church who died in the service." There was a long pause. The little fellow was somewhat bothered by her answer. Suddenly he demanded his mother's attention again. With a sense of concern—almost panic—he asked, "Mom, was that in the first or the second service?"

Why do we find this familiar story so humorous? Probably because we relate to the not-too-subtle implication that worship services are often dull and lifeless. Though Christians gather to celebrate a living God of resurrection power, the experience many times lacks energy, excitement and a sense of His divine presence. While this is not true of all churches, in general, evangelical services are weak. They fail to lead believers through a balanced and life-giving experience of corporate worship.

A.W. Tozer called worship the "missing jewel of the evangelical church." This was and still is a powerful and a tragic indictment. That which is most important is often least effective.

Author Robert G. Rayburn states,

> The worship of God is at once the true believer's most important activity and at the same time it is one of the most tragically neglected activities in the average evangelical church today. . . . There remains, however, among sincere believers . . . a woeful ignorance concerning the significance of true worship and the means of attaining the blessing of rich, rewarding corporate worship.[1]

Since Tozer's perceptive analysis was first stated, scores of pastors, teachers, professors and denominational executives have sought to give attention to this matter. New and valuable books have been published on Christian worship. Seminars are held annually across our country, aimed at improving church services. Various professional journals have dedicated entire issues to this one aspect of Christian life and ministry. More and more churches are adding ministers of music and worship to their pastoral staff. And believers are hungering for rich and dynamic worship. There is an openness toward expressing praise in new ways, toward experiencing renewal and power through corporate worship. All of this is good—very good—and it holds promise for the evangelical church.

Yet, in spite of this renewed interest and attention, most congregations are still failing miserably. They may realize the jewel is missing, but they somehow have not been able to find it.

That is the reason for this volume: to help those who read it to lay hold of this life-giving treasure called corporate worship. There are riches and benefits untold for those who draw near to God through balanced, dynamic worship. While uncovering this jewel is not easy, it can be done. Pastors and worship leaders can consistently design worship services that will be powerful and life-giving.

The material that follows was originally developed in the context of my responsibilities at Alliance Theological Seminary. However, after leaving ATS, my family and I moved to Redding, California, where we founded Risen King Community Church, a congregation of The Christian and Missionary Alliance. RKCC has served as a marvelous context for implementing the principles of worship discussed in this volume. In less than two years, Risen King Community Church has grown from a handful of committed people to a congregation numbering over 800. Dynamic corporate worship has been foundational to this remarkable growth. In addition, several principles discussed in this resource have been shaped out of my private hunger for more of God. Together, these influences have served to impact my understanding and practice of corporate worship.

What follows is not the final answer in designing dynamic worship services. In fact, the entire volume focuses more upon questions than answers—questions that should serve as the foundation for planning weekly worship services. When asked, these questions become guiding principles that will keep services both balanced and dynamic. They are principles that can help any local church get a firm grasp on this wonderful jewel called worship.

The first chapter is a discussion of the priority of worship in the body of Christ. Chapters two through six are the core, addressing the foundational questions leaders must ask when designing worship services. The summary will serve as a practical guide for implementing this material in a local church. In the Epilogue, discussion centers upon the relationship of holiness to worship, a vital lesson learned since first writing this book. Each chapter includes several discussion questions at the end. These are provided to help churches experience the wonder and power of corporate worship. If that happens, then all praise and thanks are His!

I would like to express my deep appreciation to H. Robert Cowles, retired executive vice president of Christian Publications. Bob heard my lectures at Delta Lake Bible Conference Center in Rome, New York, and encouraged me to write this book. His affirmation and guidance were critical to my completing this project.

Finally, I express my appreciation to Neill Foster, publisher of Christian Publications. He encouraged me to make important revisions to the original edition of this volume. Neill insisted that such changes would only increase the value of such a resource. I believe he was right.

I am equally indebted to my former secretary, Lois Volstad. She served as typist, proofreader and all-around cheerleader throughout. Her corrections and suggestions were always helpful. Lois went far beyond the call of duty while working on the original manuscript.

In addition, I want to thank my former administrative assistant, Shirley Hahn, who carried much of the administrative load as I wrote this book. She diligently stood guard at my office door, encouraging me to "get my work done." Shirley is a gifted servant and a true Barnabas.

Is Worship Top Priority?

L EAVING PASTORAL MINISTRY and moving into seminary education brought numerous changes for my family and me. A new home, town, community and job all presented new challenges. One of the most important of these was finding a church home—something completely new to us. For 10 years we had been a parsonage family. Now we had the burden and opportunity to select the church we would join, and it turned out to be a difficult task.

For several weeks, we visited a different church each Sunday. The entire family attended both Sunday school and morning worship. We evaluated facilities, children's and youth programs, friendliness of members and openness to visitors. Naturally, theological position was quite important, as was the church's commitment to missions and evangelism. But, believe it or not, what always topped our list was the worship service: How was the experience of corporate praise and adoration?

After each service, we asked ourselves a number of questions. Was it inspiring? Were we spiritually nourished? Did we feel free to participate? Could we sense the presence and power of God? Was Christ lifted up? Did we feel comfortable? Was there an atmosphere of celebration? No matter how the other aspects appeared, the worship service most affected our decision on whether or not to return.

This practical experience reinforced a conviction that was growing deep within me. Worship services significantly affect the growth of churches as well as the spiritual development of individual believers. When designed and led properly, worship services draw people to God and enhance spiritual maturity. When done poorly, they can be a source of decline and spiritual malnutrition.

Upon leaving seminary education, God called my family and me into church planting. With the help of my colleague, Ron Walborn, a blueprint was designed to prioritize dynamic worship in the life of this new congregation. What resulted has solidified my belief in the power of worship. Pastors and local church leaders must make worship a priority in their churches. It is a matter of life!

Invest in worship

Dr. Ray Ortlund, well-known author and founder of Renewal Ministries, insists that "Worship must be *top* priority for the local church." It is a most serious business deserving our greatest investment. Why is this? First and foremost because our worship affects God. The quality of our expression of praise represents the depth and intensity of our worship and devotion. The corporate worship service is an act of adoration in which God's people seek to please Him with praise. They seek to bless Him, honor Him, extol Him, glorify Him. God is certainly deserving of our utmost and best in worship, and local churches miss a great opportunity to bring Him glory when their worship services are shallow and directionless.

Second, corporate worship has the potential to positively

affect every believer present. Designed and led properly, the worship service can edify believers, consistently building them up in Christ Jesus. Men, women, youth and children soon anticipate weekly worship with a sense of excitement and expectation. The service becomes a place to meet God—a place to be filled, renewed and joyously sent forth. All of this and more can happen when churches make worship top priority.

Third, corporate worship services can and do affect unbelievers. Indirectly, this happens when excited and renewed Christians leave the worship service and enter the marketplace of daily living. Victory in Christ enables them to witness effectively, both in word and deed. Filled on Sunday, men and women are able to serve living water to others on Monday. This is how it can be and should be when services are properly designed. Believers can leave the service renewed, refreshed and recommitted to serve Christ in the world.

In addition, unbelievers are often directly affected by worship services. For many people, their first encounter with the Christian community is in a worship service. Invited by a friend, they observe us in our most important activity. Whether done well or not, that service leaves a lasting impression. When positive, worship convinces visitors that God is alive, powerful and, most important, relevant, often attracting unbelievers to life in the family of God. But if the experience is negative, it leaves them with the unfortunate conviction that Christianity is dull and lifeless.

In 1982 I had the opportunity to study with Dr. David Watson, former pastor of St. Michael-Le-Belfrey Parish, York, England. He came to Fuller Theological Seminary to teach an intensive course entitled "Renewal in the Local

Church." In a word, the experience was tremendous.

Accompanying Dr. Watson were several members of his ministry team from York. Each day they led in worship, using choruses, drama, special music and testimony. The team modeled the worship styles and principles of renewal that were used of God to bring new life and growth in their church. These times of worship produced the same sense of renewal in our class. My understanding of Christian worship was significantly reshaped and refreshed. Those days in Pasadena were both life-giving and life-transforming. I sensed a new power in praise and a new sense of God's presence in my life. All of this came as a result of well-balanced corporate worship.

David Watson spoke particularly about the priority of worship within the Christian community. He said that worship

- is the first and great commandment: we should love the Lord our God (Mark 12:30)
- is the first action we should take when we come into God's presence; we should "enter his gates with thanksgiving" (Psalm 100:4)
- is the first response we should make when we come to Christ: "[Offer] spiritual sacrifices acceptable to God through Jesus Christ" (1 Peter 2:5)
- is the first mark of the Holy Spirit in our lives: "God sent the Spirit of his Son into our hearts, the Spirit who calls out, 'Abba, Father' " (Galatians 4:6)
- was the first sign of the Holy Spirit at Pentecost: "All of them were filled with the Holy Spirit and began to speak in other tongues" (Acts 2:4)
- was the first priority of the early church: "They continued to meet together in the temple courts . . . praising

God" (Acts 2:41–47)

- was their first reaction when in trouble: "When they heard this, they raised their voices together in prayer to God" (Acts 4:24)
- is the first essential when listening to God: "While they were worshiping and fasting, the Holy Spirit said . . ." (Acts 13:1ff)
- is the ceaseless language of heaven: "Day and night they never stop saying: 'Holy, holy, holy' " (Revelation 4:8)

Can there be any doubt that worship should be our first concern? Is it any wonder that local churches investing in worship are experiencing renewal, power and spiritual vitality? Find a church with exciting, balanced worship, and you will find a church growing in quality and in number. The opposite is equally true. Where worship services are poorly designed, the experience can be an exhausting endurance contest. Regardless of other programs and ministries, ineffective worship will stifle growth. People will soon find reason not to attend Sunday morning.

But wherever churches and groups of Christians prioritize balanced worship, good things begin to happen. Designing and leading such services of praise and adoration should therefore be a priority of every church. They can be the doorway to renewal and blessing. Congregations cannot afford not to invest in worship. Every local church must take time to learn principles and practices of balanced corporate praise and adoration. Backed by prayer and the power of the Holy Spirit, these can be a sound prescription for church health and growth.

Negative trends affecting worship services

I have had opportunity to discuss worship with a number

of pastors, laypersons and students. Classrooms, conferences and coffee tables are great settings to feel the pulse of the church on the matter. Often people open up and share their dissatisfaction with popular practices—practices that hinder churches from experiencing dynamic worship. Several such problem areas come up repeatedly in conversation. They are mentioned often enough to be identified as the more common weaknesses in Christian worship. By discussing these hindrances to worship, we may be able to avoid problems in our own worship services.

1. *The sermon has become the most important part of the worship service.* Do not misunderstand me. I am fully committed to the Word of God and solid biblical preaching. In fact, one of my teaching assignments as a professor has been homiletics. My life and countless other lives have been transformed through preaching. It is a blessed ministry of the Christian church and should be held in high regard.

But preaching and worship are not synonymous. A worship service is much more than believers gathering to listen to the pastor preach. Unfortunately, however, in many churches the focal point of the worship service is the proclamation event. When that is so, corporate worship suffers. Anything done before the sermon becomes only a preliminary. More than a few pastors, knowingly or unknowingly, promote this by ordering their service so that the sermon is center stage—the focal point of everyone's attention.

Certainly sermons are a necessary part of balanced worship. But while they are critically important, they in no way stand alone. Each element of the service is significant and necessary to a balanced, healthy experience. When preaching dominates and overshadows all other parts of the service, it leads to serious problems. Worshipers often become primarily listeners. The evaluation of the service can be based on how good or bad the sermon was—not on the quality of worship. The goal of such a service focuses not on what people *give* but on what they *get* from the experience. A congregation easily becomes attracted to the proclaimer instead of the Proclaimed One. Moreover, when the sermon is the centerpiece, weaknesses in the pulpit are compounded.

Care must be taken to see everything we do in worship as important. We must reject the notion that what comes before the sermon are preliminaries to be covered as quickly as possible—on the way to the "good stuff." Prayer and thoughtful preparation should be put into every part of the worship service. Each activity, from prelude to benediction, should be enthusiastically embraced as vital to good worship. This does not detract from preaching. If anything, it enhances proclamation. People and pastor move to the message spiritually awake, sensitive and prepared for response. When the sermon is part of an integrated worship experience, it brings people face to face with the One who gives meaning and purpose to life.

My own experience preaching in a variety of churches, conferences and camp meetings verifies these observations. Sometimes there is little worship preceding the message. When that happens, I usually find it difficult to preach, and I find that the sermon demands great intensity. The mood is not Godward, and attention almost defies capture. On other occasions, people spend time in praise and adoration before the sermon. By the time I open the Scriptures, all is ready. Receptivity and attentiveness increase a hundredfold. People participate in the sermon as active listeners, feeding on the Word of God. These times are joyous and fruitful, and any pastor who truly loves effective preaching will find great delight in such an experience. It is there for any pastor willing to keep the focus of worship clear and well balanced. Order your service so that sermons complement worship, not substitute for worship.

2. *Pastors do too much in the worship service.* Bob's words hit me right between the eyes. He and Sue had moved into the Pennsylvania community where I was pastoring a small congregation. They began searching for a church home and came to the worship service to "check us out." As they were leaving, I made it my business to thank them for attending the morning service. I was genuinely glad they had visited and hoped they would return. After my words of welcome, Bob delivered that unforgettable response: "For a while there I wondered if you were going to come down and collect the offering, too!" In other words, "You did too much in the worship service."

Bob's stinging remark was right on! I was doing far too much in the worship service. From call-to-worship to benediction, I was the only person actively involved. On that particular Sunday I even directed the choir, and believe it or not, sang a solo for the special music.

In my desire to have all things done well, I was actually weakening the worship service. It lacked movement and variety, as well as involvement of the body. Instead of raising up leaders, I was encouraging passivity. What a disaster!

Unfortunately, this problem is not unique to me. Too many pastors are the focal point in evangelical worship services. Rather than setting gifted people free to develop as worship leaders, they hold on to the service as if it were exclusively their domain.

I see several reasons why this is so. First, it is the primary model that most pastors have seen. Many have grown up in small churches where the minister did everything. Second, some churches expect pastors to do all the ministry. With little appreciation for the call to equip servants for ministry, laypeople often conclude: "That's why we hired you—to minister." Third, many pastors are insecure about releasing laypeople for significant ministry. In some way it is perceived as a threat to their sense of worth or importance in the church.

We must go beyond pastor-centered ministry to body ministry. Nowhere is this more important than in the worship service. Lay involvement in worship can open the door to new power and excitement. And there are countless ways to mobilize people in the worship service. In chapter five we will discuss some of these ways in detail. I will make a number of suggestions to help you design services that will set laypeople free to participate and lead in worship.

3. *Attending a worship service is similar to attending the theater or a concert—it is a spectator event.* This trend grows directly from the previous one. The fewer people called on to participate, the more passive worship becomes. Those in the pews sit and watch as the person up front performs. They evaluate the service based on what they receive rather than on what they put into the experience.

Watching is commonplace in our society and comes easily to most of us. We are a generation of spectators who watch television, sports events—most everything. And this has affected our understanding of the worship service. It has become another place where we watch and where we expect to be entertained.

Several years ago I was invited to preach at a large church in Oklahoma. I will never forget the Sunday morning worship service. It was a first-class production in almost every way. The sanctuary was beautifully decorated. Two choirs and a hand bell ensemble were top quality. Ushers wore matching blazers. Stage hands dimmed lights on cue. The pastor even had a telephone hidden in a plant by his chair in case of a last-minute change in the program schedule. To say the least, the entire event was most impressive. Unfortunately, though, all the congregation did was watch. Nowhere were they called on to actively participate. In a few places they applauded, but that seemed to be in praise of the performers. For them, worship was a passive event. They were there primarily to be entertained.

How contrary to the intended purpose of worship—an activity meant to engage each person in attendance. The people on the platform are to serve as leaders—"cheerleaders" of sorts. Their purpose, far from entertaining, is to lead those present in worship. As models, they show us how. As signposts, they point us to God. No one sits and watches. Rather, all are called into action, presenting to God in songs and words their praise and expressions of devotion. The order of worship is not a program guide or schedule of events. It is a road map that leads all the assembly along the proper path of balanced, healthy worship.

4. *Worship services have become overly predictable.* There is little question but that we need both order and consistency in the worship service. Order helps the worshiper make sense of the experience. It keeps the service balanced and holistic. Consistency enables worshipers to feel comfortable in the service. They are familiar with what is happening; negative anxiety is eliminated. Nothing is worse than not knowing what comes next or what to do at a certain time.

But there is a negative side to order and consistency. When the order of worship is too predictable, worshipers can quickly lose interest. The service becomes more of the same old thing. When songs, Scripture, sermon and style are identical week after week, worship loses its excitement.

There is little sense of expectation. People no longer wonder what new way God will lead them to experience His presence and power. Soon, worship becomes boring.

A dear friend and colleague shared with me an experience he had while pastoring. Sitting up front and facing the congregation affords a pastor the opportunity to watch his people. For several weeks, Mark noticed one of his laymen marking the side of his bulletin. Curious about this routine, Mark asked what he was doing. Somewhat nervously he confessed to checking off each part of the service as it was completed.

Mark thought about this for some time. He realized that this man was sending him a clear message regarding the worship service. What Mark discovered is true in all worship. We cannot afford to do the same thing in the same way week after week. If we do, worshipers check out—if not bodily, at least mentally.

Good worship balances order and a sense of the unexpected. Worship leaders must design services that wed freedom and form, consistency and creativity. This keeps worship services fresh and full of movement and spiritual vitality. Worshipers then begin to anticipate the beginning of something new in the service, not the end of something old.

5. *Form and order in worship are often dictated purely by tradition.* In *The Problem of Wine Skins,* Howard Snyder discusses biblical structures of the church. In one particular section, he talks about the differences between temples and tabernacles. Snyder indicates that the tabernacle was God's idea. He characterizes God as "dynamic, not static, mobile, . . . a God of surprises." This is to be equally true of His people, the church. The church should be "mobile, flexible, pilgrim."

Temples, says Snyder, are man's design, not God's. Unlike tabernacles, temples are static, immovable, cold and certainly not dynamic. Snyder also reminds us that temples have been consistently destroyed throughout history.

While Snyder's main focus is not on worship, his insights have a bearing on the subject. God wants His people to be a pilgrim people, dynamic and flexible. Like the tabernacle of old, where and when the Spirit moves, we move. Where the Spirit settles, we settle. In worship, this means that form and order must be Spirit-directed and Spirit-filled.

Unfortunately, many churches have a temple mentality. Form and order are dictated by tradition and the past. At the time they were instituted, these forms were fresh and dynamic. Over the years, however, the form became stagnant and stopped generating vibrant worship. Yet, it was set in stone—a "temple." The Spirit would have had them move on to other forms, but congregations with temple mentalities do not move. They hold on to the traditions of previous generations. Because of this, worship becomes static, lifeless and immobile.

I am not advocating change for change's sake. What I am encouraging is flexibility and mobility in form and order. Our worship services should certainly be sensitive to tradition but not completely determined by tradition. Forms of worship should not be institutionalized. Instead, they should be carefully designed, consistent with the moving of the Spirit in this day—at this time and place in history. Where the Spirit rests in worship, we rest. Where and when the Spirit moves on, we move on.

6. *What happens in worship is not always relevant to daily living.* People will not embrace Christianity simply because our message is true. They want to see that our message is relevant. Does faith work in real life? Does Christianity

affect daily living in contemporary society? Is what we express and confess on Sunday relevant to life on Monday? This principle is equally true of the Christian worship service. Not only should we seek to embrace the transcendent in worship, we should also relate to the temporal. Form, order and message in worship should be relevant to the culture, language and experience of daily living. Otherwise, people will not easily integrate the experience of worship with day-to-day life.

Let me illustrate this point. For some reason, many churches have embraced classical music as the style most conducive to worship. Where people regularly and consistently listen to classical music, this is fine. But in most places this is not the case. For example, in my community 90 percent of the music purchased is contemporary of one form or another. Yet, in the majority of churches in our town, the music of worship is primarily classical. For many people, this reversal makes it difficult to relate worship to life. The experience of Sunday is foreign to life on Monday.

Music is just one example. The language used in the service, the dress, even the architecture are others. If the forms are irrelevant to daily life, worship may be unattractive and difficult to integrate with life. Though the message proclaimed is true, the medium is unfamiliar and unnatural.

Worship leaders must work hard to design services that balance the transcendent and the temporal. Care must be taken to match forms and language of worship with that of the people. The Sunday morning service should be related to and integrated with daily living. Songs, prayers, symbols and messages should be clearly understood. To achieve all of this, services must be designed with sensitivity, Spirit-guidance and a commitment to contemporary relevance.

7. *People often do not encounter God in worship.* This

problem is by far the most devastating. Sunday after Sunday, people leave church without sensing the presence of God in worship. The entire experience becomes an exercise in human effort. Where and when this is true, people leave the service much as they came in. They are unchanged, uninspired and unprepared to serve Christ in the marketplace of daily living.

A.W. Tozer referred to this in his classic, *The Pursuit of God.*

> The world is perishing for lack of the knowledge of God, and the church is famishing for want of His presence. The instant cure of most of our religious ills would be to enter the Presence in spiritual experience, to become suddenly aware that we are in God and that God is in us. This would lift us out of our pitiful narrowness and cause our hearts to be enlarged. This would burn away the impurities from our lives as the bugs and fungi were burned away by the fire that dwelt in the bush.[2]

Why do people not encounter God in worship? Many of the reasons we have already discussed. A dryness has settled over the corporate worship service. Instead of experiencing life-giving power, churches are suffering. Form and order is there, but services lack spiritual vitality and the dynamic presence of God. Services are poorly planned, lacking serious preparation and prayer. Congregations have not been taught to worship, particularly about the power of praise. Forms are often outdated, characterized by a dead traditionalism. Worst of all, many believers have accepted the power of God in theory but have rejected it in practice. Fearing wild fire, congregations have opted for no fire at all. As a result, worship lacks its most important and powerful element, God's presence.

General William Booth once said that if a church was on fire for God, people for miles around would come to see it burn. Find a church where true worship leads believers into God's presence, and you will see church growth. And, as stated earlier, find a church that lacks God's presence in worship, and you will find a church that is dying.

According to church growth analysts, most United States churches are doing just that—dying. They are dying for a fresh touch from God. Worship leaders must design services and prepare people for true worship—worship that leads everyone present into the presence of Almighty God.

Principles for renewing worship

R.B. Allen, a professor at Western Conservative Baptist Seminary, in a convincing book on the Psalms called, *Praise! A Matter of Life and Breath*, agrees that the church's understanding of worship is inadequate.

> Worship is the weakest area of evangelical Christianity. We are strongest in the areas of evangelism, teaching and fellowship. We are improving greatly in the area of servanthood (application of the gospel to social needs) and the ministry of healing (counseling and care for the emotional needs of people). But depth in the area of worship is badly lacking.[3]

Certainly the previously mentioned hindrances significantly contribute to this weakness. The discussion has not been exhaustive, but it has identified the great need. And the felt need prompts some questions—questions we should ask when designing worship services. They are questions that will serve as guiding principles of worship, keeping services balanced and life-giving. They are questions that will lead us into vital worship services.

These guiding questions embody four foundational principles basic to dynamic worship. They serve as the core for what is ahead in this volume.

1. Will this worship service glorify God?
2. Will this worship service be Christ-centered?
3. Will this worship service edify believers?
4. Will this worship service appeal to visitors?

Dynamic worship results when services are designed with these principles in mind. They serve as the measuring rod and blueprint for worship leaders. Each and every service should be designed to glorify God, to be Christ-centered, to edify believers and to appeal to visitors. Whatever is done in worship is to be influenced and shaped by these goals. The choice of songs, the time of prayer, the mode of praise, the order of service, the style of music and the form and content of the sermon must be determined by planning faithful to these four questions. Each principle should affect and be affected by the other. Interwoven, they will form a solid basis for life-giving worship. The diagram at the end of this chapter may help formulate this concept in your thinking.[4]

The rest of this book will focus upon characteristics of worship that are consistent with these four principles. When leaders address these questions as they prepare for worship, vital worship should result—worship that will glorify God, center on Christ, edify believers and appeal to visitors.

Defining worship

Before moving on, we need to define worship. Although

most Christians participate in worship services weekly, few have a clear understanding of worship. Ask believers to define worship and they will refer to attending church services, singing, praying, listening. The focus is often upon the means of worship—what people do in the service. Even pastors focus on the means of worship when preparing services. Concern almost exclusively centers on what they are going to do in worship that week. What songs, what Scriptures, what sermon, what order. When this happens, the means of worship is mistaken for the meaning of worship.

Robert Webber, in his book *Worship Old and New*, defines worship in the broadest sense as "a meeting between God and His people."

> In this meeting God becomes present to His people, who respond with praise and thanksgiving. Thus the worshiper is brought into personal contact with the one who gives meaning and purpose to life; from this encounter the worshiper receives strength and courage to live with hope in a fallen world.[5]

At the heart of this encounter with Almighty God is the people's response of praise and thanksgiving. Christians gather to lift up words, songs, prayers of praise, responding to God's self-giving and self-revelation.

When defining worship more particularly, it is helpful to look at the word's origin—its etymology. The word *worship* is a contraction of the Old English *weorthscipe*. While the spelling is unfamiliar, the word is actually worth-ship. To worship, then, is to ascribe worth to someone or something. In Christian worship that means ascribing worth to God. Believers come into His presence and actively declare His worth-ship. Ralph Martin, popular New Testament scholar, said:

> To worship God is to ascribe to Him supreme worth, for He alone is worthy.[6]

God has wonderfully blessed His people, and we in turn should lift praise and thanksgiving to His name. We gather in worship to focus our attention upon Him, declaring in every possible way His glory, His grace and His mighty deeds.

I like what Ronald Allen and Gordon Borror say about worship in their work, *Worship: Rediscovering the Missing Jewel.* They emphasize that worship is a celebration of the living God and His Christ.

> What then is the essence of worship? It is the celebration of God! When we worship Him, we celebrate Him: We extol Him, we sound His praises, we boast in Him.[7]

Worship is a glorious celebration of God and all He has done in creation and redemption. In this celebration, care is taken to offer the best in praise and adoration. From call-to-worship through the benediction, everyone present is involved, lifting before the throne an offering of praise befitting God's supreme worth.

Songs, sermons and prayers can be carefully interwoven into a glorious tapestry called worship. It is meant to be a wondrous celebration of God's self-giving in which Christians energetically declare His worth. That not only *sounds* exciting, it *is* exciting. With care, planning and clear principles, any church can design worship services that are truly celebrations of God's worth.

Discussion Questions

1. What are several reasons for making worship top priority in your local church?
2. What effect does worship have on believers? On unbelievers?
3. What problems arise when the sermon becomes the focal point of worship?
4. Can you list several effects pastor-dominated worship has upon a congregation? What are they?
5. What are some ways laypeople can be actively involved in the worship service?
6. What is the difference between a "tabernacle" and a "temple" mentality when determining forms of worship?
7. What did A.W. Tozer see as the cure of most of our religious ills? (see p. 20)
8. What four questions should guide leaders when designing worship services?
9. What is worship in the broadest sense?
10. What do Allen and Borror describe as the essence of worship? (p. 24)

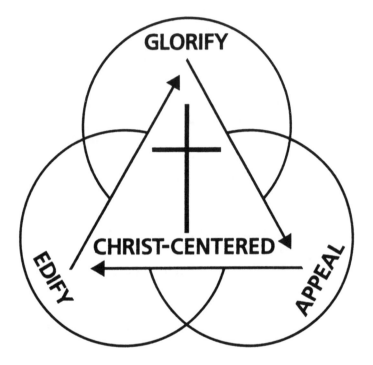

Will This Worship Service Glorify God? Part 1

ONE OF MY FAVORITE EXAMPLES of dynamic worship is in First Chronicles 15 and 16. There King David is bringing the Ark of the Covenant into Jerusalem. David wanted to establish Jerusalem as the center of civil and spiritual life for the Israelites. To accomplish this, he decided to locate the palace and the Ark of the Covenant in that city. The Ark served as a focal point of faith for the Israelites. It was a symbol of God's presence in their midst.

A great celebration took place as the Ark arrived in Jerusalem. The atmosphere was festive. There was a great procession, marked by choirs, instrumental music and an excited king dancing before the Lord. David sacrificed burnt offerings and fellowship offerings to God and blessed the people in the name of the Lord.

To Asaph, the choir director, David gave a song of praise to God that was to be part of the worship celebration. It is clear that David's goal that day was to glorify God.

Look particularly at the focus of chapter 16, verses 8–11, 23–25 and 28–29. David wrote:

Give thanks to the LORD, call on his name;
    make known among the nations what he has done.
Sing to him, sing praise to him;
    tell of all his wonderful acts.
Glory in his holy name;
    let the hearts of those who seek the LORD rejoice.
Look to the LORD and his strength;
    seek his face always.
Sing to the LORD, all the earth;
    proclaim his salvation day after day.
Declare his glory among the nations,
    his marvelous deeds among all peoples.
For great is the LORD and most worthy of praise;
    he is to be feared above all gods.
Ascribe to the LORD, O families of nations,
    ascribe to the LORD glory and strength,
    ascribe to the LORD the glory due his name.
Bring an offering and come before him;
    worship the LORD in the splendor of
        his holiness.

David wanted everyone present to know that God was powerful, wonderful and marvelous. He sang of His mighty acts and glorious deeds. He declared the Lord's strength and ascribed glory to His name. David desired all nations and people to know that "the LORD is great and most worthy of praise." This was the focal point of the entire worship celebration—bringing glory to Almighty God.

Like David's celebration in First Chronicles, all worship services should seek to bring glory to God. This is the starting place of dynamic Christian worship. Believers should gather to declare God's praise. Like David, Christians should sing of His mighty acts, tell of His glorious deeds, declare His glory before the nations. This is central to true worship.

The first question leaders must ask when designing worship services is, "Will this worship service glorify God?" In what way or ways will the congregation declare His worthship and ascribe Him glory? Choices of hymns, choruses, special music and testimonies should be made with this goal in mind. There are several characteristics of worship that glorify God—ingredients that must be present if the experience is to truly bring Him honor: (1) Worship must be sacrificial, (2) Worship must be sensible, (3) Worship must be sincere and (4) Worship must be Spirit-filled. The first two will be discussed in this chapter, the other two in chapter 3.

Worship must be sacrificial

Worship that glorifies God is sacrificial. Much is said about sacrifice in the Old and New Testaments. For the most part, that discussion will be left for biblical scholars. It does not take much scholarship, however, to build a case for worship as an offering to God. When believers gather to worship, they come to offer expressions of praise and adoration. It is a releasing on the part of the worshiper—a costly surrender that places certain demands on him or her. This offering involves a sacrifice of words, bodies and possessions to the Lord. To the extent that worship is sacrificial, it brings glory to God.

1. *Worship should be a sacrifice of our words.* The writer of Hebrews writes:

> Through Jesus, therefore, let us continually offer to God a sacrifice of praise, the fruit of lips that confess his name. (13:15)

One way Christians are to express joy and delight in God is through praise. It is the acceptable sacrifice of our lips. When Christians gather together for worship, they should lift words of praise and adoration as a sacrifice before God. It is a key part of the worship experience.

British pastor Derek Prime ably speaks of the priority of praise in a believer's life and worship. In the introduction to *Created to Praise* he writes:

> I want to try to establish the right position of praise in the Christian life, because praise occupies a unique place in God's purposes. When God first formed man, man was created to praise God; when we are born again, through faith in our Lord Jesus Christ, we are recreated in order that we may praise God.
>
> We must not be afraid to express the depths of our feelings as we worship God. If we raise our voices in praise and welcome of some important state dignitary, should we not raise our voices at the presence of the King of kings and Lord of lords? Even as there is variation in tempo and volume in a beautiful piece of music, so there will be variation in the expression of our praise to God. What is important is that we should not be inhibited in expressing sincere praise. . . . There is no danger of our being overenthusiastic in our praise of God if it is from our heart. The soul that is in love with Jesus Christ must sing! What are our lame praises in comparison to His love?[8]

Prime goes on to tell us that praise should be the believer's preoccupation—in song, in prayer, in trials, in everyday life, in death and in heaven.

Countless Scriptures give testimony to the priority of

praise for God's people. There are two that have been particularly motivating and instructive:

> But you are a chosen people, a royal priesthood, a holy nation, a people belonging to God, *that you may declare the praises* [italics mine] of him who called you out of darkness into his wonderful light. (1 Peter 2:9)

> Praise the LORD.
> Praise the LORD, O my soul.
>   I will praise the LORD all my life
>   I will sing praise to my God as long as I live.
>   (Psalm 146:1–2)

All through the Bible we see, by example and command, that praise is a characteristic of believers' worship and devotion to God.

In corporate worship, this sacrifice of praise is expressed through singing, speaking and exclamation. Each form of praise is rooted in Scripture and has been practiced throughout church history. Hymns of praise should be an integral part of the worship service. Songs and choruses need to be carefully selected, focusing on the nature and glory of God. Our singing, as the words *hymn* and *song* imply, should not only be *about* God but *to* God.

When believers lift their voices to God in sincere adoration, it seems to unleash power and excitement. Such singing should characterize the first moments of the service, setting the tone for the people as they gather in Christ's name. It prepares the congregation to enter into worship wholeheartedly and in tune with God. This, of course, presumes that worshipers commit themselves to singing to the Lord. Halfhearted, disinterested singing does not qualify as a sacrifice of praise. John Wesley once admonished worshipers:

> Sing lustily, and with a good courage . . . Beware of singing as if you were half dead or half asleep; but lift up your voice with strength. Be no more afraid of your voice now, nor more ashamed of its being heard, than when you sang the songs of Satan.[9]

Worshipers should also be given opportunity to speak words of praise to God. This can be done in several ways. Leaders could include a time in the service for sentence prayers and praises. Believers would be encouraged to lift aloud a brief sentence about God's mercy and grace. These sentences may be from Scripture or a short, spontaneous word of thanks for a recent blessing. At first people may be hesitant, but with proper guidance they will soon join in with a "sacrifice of praise." The word sacrifice is appropriate, in that most people will not find it easy to give such expressions.

Another way to include words of praise is through an occasional time of testimony in the service. Pre-select individuals to share a word of praise regarding God's intervention in their lives. This must be carefully guided, so that it does not become too long or aimless. Through this, God's glory will be declared as a fact of our present experience, not just a record of history.

Finally, congregations would do well to learn the value of shouting God's praises as a sacrifice of worship. This may sound radical, yet it is a thoroughly biblical practice. In *Praise: A Way of Life*, Paul Hinnebusch writes:

> There is no doubt that the Hebrew people were often quite loud in their praise of God. This is clear from two

Hebrew words which occur frequently in the psalms, *ruwa* and *teruwah*. Figuratively, *ruwa* means "to split the ears with sound; that is *to shout* (for alarm or joy); to make a joyful noise." "Make a joyful noise to God, all the earth" (Psalm 66:1). "Shout to God with loud songs of joy" (Psalm 47:1).

From this verb is derived the noun *teruwah*, which means "clamor, that is, acclamation of joy, or a battle cry." "Blessed are the people who know the festal shout (*teruwah*)" (Psalm 89:15).

When the Hebrew psalms were translated into Latin, these two words were rendered as *jubilare* and *jubilation*, from which our word "jubilation" is derived.[10]

Our excitement and confidence in the Lord should give us reason for shouting. In my congregation, we learned the festal shout "The Lord Reigns!" From time to time we would lift up needs and concerns before one another. At the end, I would lead as we then shouted, "The Lord Reigns!" It was a declaration of God's trustworthiness in the midst of trial.

People in the church grew to love this practice, because it became a reminder of God's greatness and power. When I left that church, several people presented me with plaques and banners bearing the words, "The Lord Reigns!" Everywhere I share this practice, people respond positively. Such a festal shout can bring great glory to God. It also instills a renewed faith among God's people. Congregations would do well to embrace this ancient and biblical form of worship.

2. *Worship that glorifies God involves a sacrifice of our bodies.* This point consistently draws the most reaction from people. In many evangelical churches we are not yet ready to use our bodies in worship. Fearing wild fire or "charis-

mania," believers are encouraged to remain as reserved as possible in their expressions of praise. Clapping, lifting hands or body motion of any kind is almost taboo. This is unfortunate. Why? First, because body language is recognized as a powerful means of communication. Second, restricting bodily responses can be stifling to some worshipers, just as demanding outward expressions of praise would be threatening to others. Third, and most important, closing the door to clapping, lifting hands or other types of body movement is not consistent with scriptural practices of worship.

One way Scripture talks about using our bodies in worship is through lifting hands in praise. Unfortunately, many evangelicals think this practice began with Pentecostalism. At the least, they consider it uncomfortably demonstrative.

More than once when I have taught on this subject, individuals have confronted me later. Their complaint is always the same. "Doesn't this practice lead to excesses— people drawing attention to themselves?" Of course there is that risk. But everything and anything we do as Christians, unchecked, can lead to excesses. That, however, should not cause believers to miss the blessing and meaning of such a valid expression of Christian worship.

Numerous Scriptures address this issue. Of particular note is Psalm 141:1–2.

> Oh LORD, I call to you; come quickly to me.
>   Hear my voice when I call to you.
> May my prayer be set before you like incense;
>   may the lifting up of my hands be like the evening
>   sacrifice.

Or consider Psalm 63, where David seeks to praise God in

song. In verses 2–5 he says,

> I have seen you in the sanctuary
> and beheld your power and your glory.
> Because your love is better than life,
> my lips will glorify you.
> I will praise you as long as I live,
> and in your name I will lift up my hands.
> My soul will be satisfied as with the richest of foods;
> with singing lips my mouth will praise you.

David is overwhelmed with the power and glory of God. In response, he offers songs and sacrifices of praise to Him. One expression of adoration and praise is his lifting of hands before God.

How well I remember discussing this issue with several pastors at a district conference. For the most part, the men were open. They realized that their own worship services were hurting, in need of renewal and refreshing. But one fellow just could not break through his preconceived prejudice. To him, the only time people should lift their hands in church is when there is something in them—a broom, a hammer, a paintbrush. Anything else, particularly in worship, is unnecessary and leads to problems.

After several conversations, I was asked to structure a worship service that would lead to God-glorifying praise. Excited about the opportunity, I worked with another pastor to organize a balanced, meaningful service. We offered God a sacrifice of praise through song and testimonies. Following a lengthy prayer of confession, I encouraged all those present to express their praise to God through their bodies. At first almost everyone was hesitant and self-conscious. But as we sang several choruses of praise, numerous people began to lift their hands in worship. It was not at all showy or excessive—simply God's people expressing to God their praise and adoration. As this happened, God's Spirit began to move. People had opened up, and in response, God came rushing in. I looked over at the man who had been the most negative. He was not lifting his hands, but it was obvious that God was deeply touching him. Following the service, he said nothing to me—positive or negative. But we both knew that God had met him there and that he would never again be the same.

Think for a moment about what the lifting of hands means in our culture. It is a sign of surrender. Even children know what to do when someone says "Stick 'em up." How appropriate to symbolize our surrender to God in such a natural and familiar way.

Lifting hands upward is also a way that children request things from their parents. It is a symbol of dependence. In worship, it can represent our need of God and our desire for more of Him.

Arms stretched upward can mean "lift me" or "hold me." When my children were very small, they would often greet me at the door with their arms lifted up. I knew exactly what that meant. They wanted me to pick them up and hug them. How fitting to express that same hunger to our Heavenly Father.

So there can be great meaning to this bodily expression of praise. By it worshipers express surrender, dependence and a desire to be drawn closer to God.

In summation, worship that glorifies God is not just cerebral. It is also physical. Scripture and history testify to the importance of offering to God a sacrifice of praise that engages not only the mind but the body. Worship leaders interested in dynamic services of praise must move people, in both understanding and practice, to engage their whole persons in praise.

3. *Worship should also be a sacrifice of our possessions.* Early in my ministry I became concerned about our treatment of the offering in worship. In many churches, the offering does not seem to fit into the worship service. For some, it is an interruption that gives opportunity for announcements or chatting with one's neighbor. Often it is a place for listening to special music while ushers pass the plates. In other churches it is seen as a collection for church projects and expenses. Worshipers often dislike offering time because it seems to be another "push for money"—something for which many churches are notorious. In response to these misunderstandings, many churches have eliminated the offering from the order of service, choosing rather to place plates at the back of the church. Believers can then leave an offering at their convenience as they enter or exit. While I appreciate the effort, even that practice misses the point.

Some of my experiences in black churches have helped me prioritize the place of the offering. In one, believers were encouraged to personally carry their offerings to the front. As individuals marched—almost danced—up to the altar, the congregation sang songs of praise and shouted words of adoration to God. The offering was not quickly dispensed with, but it had a significant place in the service.

In a black church in Harlem, the church elders took their places beside a four-foot-tall, hollow cross. Worshipers brought their gifts forward, placing them inside the cross as an act of surrender. In a deeply meaningful way, this linked sacrificial giving with God's self-giving on Calvary.

Two concepts can help us put the offering in its proper perspective. First, it is an offering and not a collection. The goal is not to gather funds but to present God with a sacrifice of our possessions. It is to represent the offering of our lives to Him. As an act of worship, it symbolizes the full and total sacrifice of all we are and have to God. As such, it should not be preceded by a disclosure of financial needs or pleas for generosity. Rather, our gifts should flow from our recognition of God and His grace.

Second, the offering should be seen as a response to God's self-giving. Because of what God has done for us, we respond in an act of surrender and dependence. Our giving flows from God's giving to us. Thus it is an expression of praise. The offering cannot be randomly scheduled in the service. It should follow a time of praising God and hearing His Word. It can be most meaningful when received before the benediction. Coming at the end, the offering provides an opportunity for response to all that God has done and said in the service. The people have praised, confessed and heard from God through His Word. Now, in final response, they give to Him an offering—symbolic of their thanks and total surrender.

This concept may not be embraced without careful instruction. From my experience, however, people are ready to accept a more balanced and biblical understanding of what happens in their worship service. The benefits of this perspective are many, including better worship and more sacrificial giving to the Lord.

Worship must be sensible

Worship that glorifies God is not only sacrificial, it is also sensible. Our God is a God of order and purpose. Everything in creation fits into a specific place in a specific way and has a specific purpose. If we are going to glorify Him, our worship must be the same. Services must be designed as an intelligent, meaningful response to His self-giving. They cannot be an emotional free-for-all or a collection of unrelated acts. God-glorifying worship makes sense. It is balanced and full of meaning with a specific purpose and goal in mind.

In giving seminars on worship, I have found that many people react to the section on sacrifice, particularly the discussion regarding the use of our bodies in worship. Immediately the seminar is polarized. One group fears excesses. They argue that such an emphasis could lead to chaos, with every worshiper doing his or her own thing at any time or place in the service. Images of arms waving, people drawing attention to themselves and interrupted sermons cause great anxiety.

The other group, predisposed to a freer style of worship, sees these expressions as the answer to all their worship ills. "All our church needs is freedom to worship aggressively," they exclaim. They are ready to immediately return to their churches and demonstrate their new-found freedom. Upon hearing this, the first group is all the more convinced that bodily expressions of praise can cause real problems. Because of these tendencies, I have learned to move immediately into this section, which encourages order and sensibility in worship.

Long ago, in a letter to the Corinthian church, Paul spoke out against imbalance and chaos in worship. His concern was that the Corinthians' worship was disorderly, confusing and lacking direction. Paul's admonition was an appeal to order and clarity. That concern still remains and should be a standard for all worship services. Imbalance and disorder are unhealthy and unappealing. Worse, they do not bring glory to God.

Christian worship is not meant to be an empty, subjective high, full of energy but lacking substance. Worship is a deeply meaningful act, carefully planned and carried out. Every form must be full of meaning, placed in the service where it best complements the whole experience. What we do in worship must grow out of scriptural imperative, instruction or example. While there should be a degree of freedom, each expression must have meaning and be exercised within stated limits. And worship leaders must work hard to preserve order and balance. It is the only way worshipers can fully benefit from the worship service.

I would suggest several balances critical to orderly and sensible worship:

1. *Let the worship service be a balanced appeal to the mind, the heart and the spirit.* The late William Temple, archbishop of Canterbury, once wrote:

> Worship is the submission of all our nature to God. It is the quickening of conscience by his holiness; the nourishment of mind with his truth; the purifying of imagination by his beauty; the opening of the heart to his love; the surrender of the will to his purpose—and all this gathered in adoration, the most selfless emotion of which our nature is capable.[11]

Temple's emphasis is upon a full-orbed experience. Worship should engage and affect every part of our being. Our minds must be enlightened, our hearts stirred and our spirits quickened. Worshipers should be fed at every level. Overemphasis or absence at any level leaves the worshiper incomplete. Some services are heavily instructive but fail to inspire. Others engage the emotion with wonderful music and singing but lack depth and substance. Still others are incomplete in that they do not draw the person Godward, deeply engaging the spiritual side. Leaders must work for balance, checking regularly for unhealthy tendencies or excesses. You cannot just preach, just teach, just sing or just pray. Worshipers need a balanced diet, and it is the obligation of leaders to provide a good, healthy meal.

2. *Worship services should balance order and freedom—structure with flexibility.* You probably have experienced excesses on both sides of this issue. Some churches feel it is super-spiritual to throw out bulletins, orders of worship and sermon notes. Their goal is to be completely Spirit-led and Spirit-directed. All limits are removed, giving the Holy Spirit freedom to do whatever He wills, wherever, whenever and through whomever. While that may sound good, such services tend toward imbalance, often degenerating into an emotional end in themselves, rather than a means to an end. Sermons often go on and on without saying much. Testimonies can easily become self-serving. Singing substitutes for a genuine moving of God, appealing to emotions yet not really feeding the spirit.

The notion that the Spirit works best in unplanned, unlimited services is false. Actually, the Spirit can and does anoint planning and preparation as well as practice. Leaders do not need to wait until Sunday morning to perceive the Spirit's direction. He will reveal Himself in the preparation process, enabling worshipers to maximize their time before Him corporately. As one pastor commented, "There may be a need for more freedom in worship, but without planning there is seldom much worship in that freedom."

But the other extreme is equally disastrous. In some churches there is little or no room for spontaneity or individual expression. The service is tightly planned, with every minute filled. Leaders know *what* is happening and *where* it is to happen throughout the service. And, of course, if it is not planned, it just does not happen. It is good to plan, and order does bring meaning, but without a certain degree of freedom, we can limit the Spirit's work. Worshipers are not going to experience that unexpected and unpredictable activity of God.

We need to balance order and freedom. Leaders should carefully plan their services, building block upon block. But within the order, plan some freedom. Structure in time for the unexpected. Consider opening your prayer time for spontaneous praise words. Be open to sing an additional chorus or hymn, as led by the Spirit. Be prepared to wait in silence before the Lord, allowing Him to speak to the congregation through a Scripture, admonition, or insight spontaneously laid upon the heart of a Spirit-directed church leader. Occasionally free up time for brief words of testimony. The possibilities are limitless. Planned spontaneity can open the door to excitement and expectation within the worship service.

3. *Learn to balance liturgy with life.* The dictionary defines liturgy as "prescribed forms or ritual for public worship." Every congregation has a certain way or ways in which they worship—certain forms commonly used in their weekly celebrations of God. It may not be high church, but every congregation follows a certain liturgy or ritual. Ask regular worshipers, and they can list several forms of worship regularly practiced in their church. The purpose is, of course, consistency, linking each service with experiences and truths from the past. This is necessary so that churches do not go out on tangents or become imbalanced in theology or experience.

But for many churches, these forms or rituals are lifeless. They have become routine and empty. Consequently, leaders must work diligently to keep life in their liturgy. Every form of worship is to be a channel for the Holy Spirit.

If something has become routine, it must be renewed, reshaped or replaced. Never allow anything to become overly predictable. Careful planning can keep your liturgy fresh and meaningful. As such, forms of worship are capable of deeply affecting the worshiper through the power of the Holy Spirit.

4. *Balance the ageless experience of encountering God with forms of worship relevant to this time and place.* Worship is neither pop nor faddish. It is not some new idea of the "now" generation. Worship is as old as humankind. Throughout the ages, men and women have responded to God's self-giving through sacrifice, praise and adoration. Any experience of worship today should be significantly influenced by the past. Form, order and praise should be founded upon and shaped by the model of yesteryear. This helps today's worshiper stay theologically and historically sound.

At the same time, though, the experience of worship must make sense to today's worshiper. Too often we have not only embraced the truth or practice of a previous generation, we have also held on to the language. As a result, today's worshiper has difficulty relating to the experience. For example, it is an ageless truth that worshipers should address God with respect and honor. In previous generations, that involved the use of Thee and Thou pronouns. The truth of respect remains, but "Thee" and "Thou" are no longer relevant in most settings. To insist on their use can make it difficult for average worshipers to integrate the worship experience with daily life. The same kind of change can be seen in styles of music, praise, dress and liturgy. Leaders must balance these concerns. What we do in worship should be linked with the past yet be relevant to today's world, today's experience, today's language.

5. *Worship services should maintain a balance between*

solemnity and celebration. In some churches, worship is like a festival. There is high energy, color, movement and sound. The experience is certainly dynamic, but it often lacks depth. Worshipers leave excited (or possibly exhausted!), but the deeper issues of life have not been addressed. Those painful concerns of day-to-day living have not been uncovered. The focus of the service has been purely emotional, seeking to generate some kind of a "high."

In other settings, the atmosphere is almost funereal. The mood is hyper-solemn, the tone somber. Problems are emphasized, burdens are highlighted and facial expressions are almost painful. Congregational singing, far from raising the dead, seems like an invitation to a deeper slumber. Instead of victorious praise, you conclude that if God is indeed alive, He has not done anything significant around there for a long, long time.

Worship services should balance the costs of discipleship with the joys of Christian living; the cross with the empty tomb; the realities of battle with the confidence of victory; the deep inner hurts of people with the wholeness available in Christ; the need for confession of sin with the assurance of forgiveness; the reality of death with the promise of eternal life. Balanced worship services are in creative tension between solemnity and celebration. There are times of quiet and seasons of praise. Believers are led to repent and encouraged to rejoice.

There are, of course, other important balances. But these mentioned are the ones most crucial to order and sensibility in worship. Commitment to order and balance is a commitment to glorify God in worship. The service will have direction, meaning and purpose. Worshipers will find the experience sensible and edifying, which in turn encourages deeper involvement and integration in the life of the believer. Leaders must understand, commit themselves to and develop solid worship services. This is the standard of praise and adoration that brings God the glory due His Name.

Discussion Questions

1. Read First Chronicles 16:8–36. What do you see as the overarching theme of this psalm?
2. Name several ways in which your congregation declares the glory of God in the weekly worship service.
3. List several ways in which worshipers can offer a sacrifice of praise in your service.
4. What is your congregation's attitude toward body language such as raising hands in worship? Is their attitude biblical and balanced?
5. What changes in understanding should you work for in your church? What may be the best way to address these needs?
6. Since there are risks involved in encouraging certain forms of worship, can anything be done to keep change balanced? If so, what?
7. How do most people in your church view the offering?
8. What can be done to make the offering more worshipful and meaningful?
9. What balances do you feel are critical to orderly worship services?
10. What can leaders do to balance order and freedom? liturgy and life? the agelessness of God and relevance in space and time? solemnity and celebration?

CHAPTER

3

Will This Worship Service Glorify God? Part 2

WORSHIP THAT IS PLEASING and acceptable to God flows from the heart. It is not just a matter of correct forms, adequate energy or high levels of enthusiasm. To bring God glory, worship must be the fruit of deep inward dedication on the part of worshipers. Outward expressions must be honest representations of inner convictions and commitments of the heart. In other words, *worship that glorifies God must be sincere.*

Worship must be sincere

In their book, *Worship: Rediscovering the Missing Jewel,* Allen and Borror remind us that:

> the lesson which seems to require constant rediscovery is the fact that worship is not primarily a state of the art, but rather a state of the heart . . . by state of the heart we mean the driving desire behind the worship life of the believer.[12]

Allen and Borror are not speaking against art forms in

worship. Rather they confirm for us the priority of genuine commitment to Christ as prerequisite to true worship. It is not enough that people gather to sing, pray, listen to sermons and present offerings. People must have hearts truly surrendered to God.

If there is any question about this "matter of the heart," Scripture quickly clears it up. Look at just a few of hundreds of verses that speak to the issue.

> Love the LORD your God with all your heart and with all your soul and with all your strength. These commandments that I give you today are to be upon your hearts. (Deuteronomy 6:5–6)

> The LORD does not look at the things man looks at. Man looks at the outward appearance, but the LORD looks at the heart. (1 Samuel 16:7)

> Create in me a pure heart, O God,
>   and renew a steadfast spirit within me. (Psalm 51:10)

> Above all else, guard your heart,
>   for it is the wellspring of life. (Proverbs 4:23)

> Blessed are the pure in heart,
>   for they will see God. (Matthew 5:8)

> God is the strength of my heart
>   and my portion forever. (Psalm 73:26b)

Jesus was critical of shallow religiosity. He continually condemned the Pharisees for self-righteousness and hypocrisy. He referred to them as whitewashed tombs, appearing clean and attractive, yet inwardly lifeless and decaying. Jesus clearly demonstrated that God neither accepted nor condoned outward piety absent of inner purity. Neither robes nor greetings, fastings nor prayer, offerings nor ashes would ever substitute for a heart fixed on Him. What was true then remains true now and forever. Worship that glorifies God must spring from hearts fully dedicated to Him.

There are several ways to impact worshipers, convincing them to worship God sincerely and wholeheartedly.

1. *Be sure your congregation is openly and actively exposed to the gospel of Jesus Christ.* People need to regularly hear the call to full surrender to His Lordship. This keeps believers updated in their commitment. At the same time, it challenges the nominal Christian to express true faith in Christ. Regular reminders and gospel-centered messages keep this matter of heart commitment clear. And worshipers will not easily fall into a form of godliness absent of its power. Every regular attendant knows full well that it is not outward actions but heart faith that qualifies a person as a true believer and thus, as a true worshiper.

2. *Regularly include time for confession in the worship service.* Believers often approach worship with sin in their hearts. At some time and in some way, they have fallen short of God's glory. Such lapses serve to block the Spirit's flow in a person's life, hindering genuine worship. No matter what else is happening, the worshiper is not fully open to the Spirit's work. By scheduling a time for confession, leaders provide worshipers with the opportunity for breakthrough and cleansing. It can be an invitation to a sincere, wholehearted encounter with God.

I am not necessarily advocating public confession or even audible prayers of confession. Simply provide a time for quiet confrontation before God. Suggest possible problem areas, encouraging those in attendance to confess their sins and failures before the worship time moves on to praise and adoration. It is particularly helpful to schedule this early in the service, thereby enabling worshipers to better experience and participate in the service.

3. *To facilitate sincere worship, teach your people to prepare for worship.* Most, if not all, of us take time to prepare physically for the Sunday service. We want to be sure our clothes are neat and clean and well coordinated. Our hair has to be just so. Appearance matters, and we do whatever possible to look good for church. This is fine and certainly should be encouraged. But are we equally concerned that we be prepared spiritually for worship?

Most people rush into worship, hoping to "get into it" once in the pew. Busy weekends and busy Sunday mornings often keep people from focusing on Christ in worship. Realizing this, leaders must instruct people in ways to move from scattered-mindedness to single-mindedness—from self-centeredness to Christ-centeredness. Or, in the words of Scripture, we must teach people to "fix [their] eyes on Jesus" (Hebrews 12:2) in preparation for worship.

Encourage families and individuals to free up some quality time on Saturday evenings for spiritual preparation. David and Karen Mains call this "restoring the Sabbath."[13] Breaking away from normal activities to get quiet before the Lord can significantly enhance Sunday worship. A time of prayer, reflection, Scripture reading and praise can help people prepare to meet God. Instead of clogging their minds with television or games, they should be encouraged to center their hearts on God.

Personally, I have found our Saturday evening prayer and praise service at the seminary a wonderful way to prepare for Sunday morning worship. Since we began that weekly meeting, I have experienced a new power in the Sunday morning services. Saturday evenings now complement rather than contradict Sunday worship. Certainly such a commitment takes discipline and support, but with thoughtful teaching and innovative ideas, leaders can influence worshipers to invest in Sunday preparation.

Practical instruction is a good way to start. Laying out clothes on Saturday evening can give extra time Sunday morning for quiet preparation—so can bathing children, preparing for breakfast and setting out keys, Bibles, wallets. All of this helps people to avoid the normal Sunday morning rush. They are able to approach worship with minds focused rather than frenzied.

My family has found that listening to praise albums as we dress ministers to our spirits. Songs of worship seem to refresh and prepare us for the service. Our hearts are tuned into God, and we enter the sanctuary ready for praise. It may be a simple thing to do, but we have found that it pays great dividends. More than once I have found myself humming one of the songs as I drive to church. What a great change from the normal frustrations and anxieties of our old "hurried" pace. Quality praise music prepares the heart to encounter and embrace God's Spirit in worship.

God is willing to fill our hearts with His love and His Spirit as we gather in worship. But before He can fill us up, we need to empty ourselves out. We must confess and deal with sin. We must discipline our preoccupation and scattered-mindedness. Then our hearts can be truly focused on Him. Helping people to center in on Christ will significantly affect what they bring to and take from worship. Leaders must build up believers, encouraging them to love God with whole hearts. When this happens, the worship service will no longer be a quick fix or an experience in shallow religiosity. Worship will become a sincere overflowing of praise from the heart. That kind of worship truly brings glory to God.

Worship must be Spirit-filled

If the Holy Spirit withdrew from your worship services, would people notice? Or would the service go on much the same? A.W. Tozer, commenting on the church's need for an outpouring of the Holy Spirit, observed that if the Spirit did withdraw, most of what goes on in the church would not change. Why? Because too much of what the local church does is not empowered by the Spirit of God. There may be much activity, energy and even enthusiasm, but one critical element is missing—the power of the Holy Spirit. And without the Spirit, all activity is empty and vain.

Fundamental to Christian experience and theology is the person and work of the Holy Spirit. There is general agreement that the Holy Spirit is the agent of any and all fruit in Christian life and ministry. We may be channels of the Spirit's power and work, but He alone truly builds the kingdom of God. It is the Spirit who empowers believers to be effective in the Lord's service. He works to convict of sin, change lives and motivate people for service. He touches the hearts of men and women, drawing them to God. The Spirit may use our words, our programs, our ministries, but He and He alone does the work. When the Spirit is not present, no matter what our work may be, we are ineffective. All our efforts will not make any real or eternal difference in the scope of things.

If our worship services are to glorify God, they must be Spirit-led, Spirit-empowered and Spirit-filled. We need His power to anoint our worship so that it will be a pleasing offering to God. And certainly it is the Spirit who will ultimately work in worship to convince, convict, confirm and commit people before the Almighty God. Without His presence in worship, services will be severely limited in their impact. Pastors and church leaders must recognize this and seek the Spirit's anointing on their planning and preparation of worship services.

Early in my Christian walk, I became convinced that most believers experience little of the Holy Spirit's power in their lives and ministry. I read in Acts of signs, wonders and miracles occurring continually. Believers preached and prayed with astonishing power, boldness and effectiveness. In spite of intense opposition and persecution, they lived victorious and fruitful lives. They were, as Scripture says, "filled with the Holy Spirit." That empowerment made all the difference in their lives.

Looking at my own life, I saw a real lack of power and victory. Though serving God faithfully, I could not say I was serving Him effectively. This led me to a personal search through the Scriptures and to a time of protracted prayer for the Spirit's infilling spoken of in God's Word. No longer satisfied with ministering in my power, I wanted to live, walk and serve in His power. Without detailing all the events that followed, I will just say that God answered that prayer. He quickened my life in such a way that every aspect of my faith took on a new power—His power. I was particularly excited—and still am—about a new effectiveness in service. What a joy to discover that there was more, so much more, to effective Christian living than I had been experiencing.

This truth relates directly to church worship services. Many local churches are experiencing far less of God's power than is available. For a variety of reasons, churches have, in the words of Dr. Martyn Lloyd-Jones, become "content with something which is altogether less than intended for us."[14] Rather than their overflowing with the power of the Holy Spirit, church services are often dry and unsatisfying. We may entertain, even inspire people, but in far too many services, there is not that overwhelming encounter with God through the power of the Holy Spirit.

Obviously, there is no one-two-three formula for Spirit-filled worship. But for those who are unsatisfied and hungering for more, there are some important first steps to take. Following these steps in the churches I have served has placed us on the threshold of power in worship. I feel confident they can do the same for any body of believers. Churches can move beyond human activity to a divine encounter that leaves worshipers eternally grateful and transformed.

1. *Worship leaders and pastors must diligently pray for God to fill their services with the Spirit's power.* Scripture instructs believers to pray, promising that God is faithful to answer those who turn to Him. Our Lord said,

> Ask and it will be given to you; seek and you will find; knock and the door will be opened to you. For everyone who asks receives; he who seeks finds; and to him who knocks, the door will be opened. (Luke 11:9–10)

What a gracious promise of God! Diligent prayer does make a difference. In this case, it can make a difference in the outpouring of the Holy Spirit upon a local worship service. Fervent prayer can unleash the Spirit's presence and power in our midst.

Jesus specifically referred to the gift of the Holy Spirit as an example of answered prayer.

> Which of you fathers, if your son asks for a fish, will give him a snake instead? Or if he asks for an egg, will give him a scorpion? If you then, though you are evil, know how to give good gifts to your children, how much more will your Father in heaven give the Holy Spirit to those who ask him! (11:11–13)

God is eager to fill us with His Spirit! Scripture tells us that He is willing to pour out power in our services if we sincerely ask.

Frustrated by the lack of power in worship in my first pastorate, I felt God leading me to begin a Saturday evening prayer meeting. The purpose was to pray for the Spirit's infilling and anointing upon our worship services. Tired of the status quo, I wanted more, and my people wanted more. At first, only a handful came to pray. But God was faithful, blessing our times of prayer. The Spirit anointed our meetings, and soon people were refreshed and filled with His power. The group grew in number and in commitment to seeking God's power in worship.

Within a short time, the Saturday evening "revival" spilled over to Sunday worship. People began commenting on a new sense of God's presence, a new excitement and a new power. Worshipers came anticipating great things and offered more energetic praises to God. Soon attendance began to increase. New people were coming and finding Christ in the midst of dynamic worship.

I initiated the same type of group in my second church. There, too, it was easy to see the relationship of growth in the church to fervent prayer for God's infilling presence. Admittedly, we initiated many changes and programs to enhance growth. But these were merely channels. It was the Holy Spirit who brought renewal, flooding these channels with His power. Do you want to break through to Spirit-filled worship? The first step is prayer.

2. *Take Paul's admonition in First Thessalonians 5:9 seriously, "Do not put out the Holy Spirit's fire."* In theory, every believer wants to be Spirit-filled and Spirit-led. But practically, we are not so inclined. Most people—pastors and worship leaders included—want to worship within their own comfort zone. Also, we want to be able to control what is happening in worship. Whatever is uncomfortable or out of our hands is generally unwelcome. This limits the work of the Holy Spirit.

I have found that the Holy Spirit constantly moves people beyond their present levels of understanding and comfort. This moving is often accompanied by fear, and it demands trust and a degree of letting go. It also demands an open mind and heart—a willingness to learn new things. Anthony Campolo reminds us that the Holy Spirit always moves people beyond the status quo. He writes:

> The Spirit disrupts the old order of things and ushers in a new openness. The Spirit is new wine in the old wineskins and the new cloth on the old garment. Those who want everything to remain as it was ought not to get involved with the things of the Spirit, because the ministry of the Spirit makes all things new.[15]

I have met many people who limit the Spirit's work. Unwilling to let go, they often close their minds and hearts to everything beyond their present experience. Not only are they unwilling to be led into new truth, they often speak out against certain practices. They may cloak their comments in the guise of biblical faithfulness, but in truth the issue is control and comfort. When this happens, the Spirit's fire is quenched. Rejecting or closing our minds to new truth can stifle the Spirit's work in a congregation.

To glorify God, worship leaders must learn to be more open. While remaining rooted in Scripture and committed to balance, we need to set the Spirit free to do whatever He chooses. Though powerful, the Holy Spirit is also sensitive and gentle. What He does and teaches enhances growth and produces health. It is *our* reactions and imbalances that divide. Learn to accept His fire as a gift. Grounded in His Word and backed by prayer, unleash the Spirit from chains of unbelief. He will respond by releasing a new power and effectiveness in worship.

3. *Be careful not to grieve the Holy Spirit.* Paul warns us of this in Ephesians. In his admonition for us to live as children of light, he says,

> And do not grieve the Holy Spirit of God, with whom you were sealed for the day of redemption. (4:30)

Paul follows this instruction with the various types of sin that must be eliminated from our lives—sins that break our relationship with God and with others. The implication is obvious. Sin in our lives grieves the Holy Spirit, causing us to miss His fullness and power.

If a congregation expects to experience Spirit-filled worship, its leaders must understand the importance of repentance and confession. The Spirit will not bless where unconfessed sin remains unaddressed. This is true of individual and corporate sin. Leaders must be godly examples, seeking to live in purity and harmony with others. Corporately, congregations must dwell in unity, encouraging one another, seeking each other's best. Gossip, bitterness, anger and unforgiveness invite the Holy Spirit's rebuke rather than His blessing. Practices in worship, too, must be balanced and biblical. Pride, drawing attention to ourselves and hypocrisy are barriers to the fullness of the Spirit. All must be done in order and to the glory of God.

To avoid problems, leaders must constantly emphasize repentance, righteousness and unity. Times of confession must be incorporated into church life. Worshipers should be called to self-examination, understanding that sin affects not only their lives but the entire church body. Without a commitment to holiness, leaders cannot expect the congregation to move ahead in the Spirit's fullness and power.

The Holy Spirit makes all the difference. His presence in worship makes every service life-changing. People, conditioned by the predictable, are suddenly transformed by God's eternal power. Spirit-filled worship evokes heartfelt praise, resulting in deeper devotion and dedication to Christ. There is much more to worship than most churches are experiencing. Leaders must translate their hunger for dynamic worship into action—the action of prayer, the attitude of openness and the appeal to purity and righteousness. Doing this will put churches on the threshold of unbelievable tomorrows in worship.

Worship and Spiritual Warfare

News of Jodie's accident came just moments before our worship service was to begin. People sat in hushed silence as the details unfolded. This lovely young woman had been severely injured in an automobile accident, and was hospitalized with multiple fractures and internal injuries. Jodie was in a coma, her life hanging in the balance.

The announcement hit hard, leaving everyone deeply concerned. In a normal context, this kind of news would cast a sobering shadow upon the service, leaving worshipers so preoccupied that they would find it difficult to participate. But instead it caused the congregation that morning to be all the more aggressive in their expressions of praise. Engaging body and soul, worshipers boldly announced God's praise and declared the glory of His character.

These worshipers had been taught a very important spiritual principle. Worship is a powerful weapon against the lies and deceit of Satan. By declaring the praise of God, men and women mount an invasion of light against the evil one, dispelling darkness and welcoming God's presence in their midst. Worship pushes back the forces of the enemy, placing God's people in position to receive reconciliation, healing, deliverance and direction. In point of fact, worship is warfare!

In October, 1988, Professor Tim Warner of Trinity Evangelical Divinity School lectured at Fuller Theological Seminary on the theme, "Power Encounter and World Evangelization." As the title suggests, Warner addressed the issue of spiritual warfare with reference to Third World evangelization. Most interesting was his discussion of Satan's purpose, prior to and following his expulsion from the presence of God. Warner, basing his discussion primarily on Ezekiel 28, argued that, before his fall, Satan was appointed as worship leader in God's holy presence. Yet, growing full of pride, he desired to receive for himself the glory due God alone, and was subsequently expelled from heaven.

The biblical record emphasizes Satan's extreme jealousy and hatred of God and his ongoing desire to receive undeserved glory and praise. Denied that possibility, Satan has dedicated himself to deflect rather than reflect the glory of God. And there are two ways in which the enemy seeks to accomplish his wicked purpose. First, by lies and deceit he endeavors to keep people from focusing upon the true nature of God. Satan works to create a negative caricature of God as a wrathful ogre, turning people away from Him. Second, he wants to mar and degrade God's image within people by keeping them in bondage to sin. By these tactics Satan is able to hold people in a state of brokenness, blinded to God's true purposes, unaware of the power available to live in wholeness and harmony with Him. And as long as Satan draws attention away from God's holy nature and glory, people will remain self-centered and broken.

This truth has direct bearing upon the topic of corporate worship. Robert Webber suggests that worship is "the work of God's people." What is that all-important work which believers are to do? I would submit that the work of worship includes "declaring the glory of God" in opposition to the forces of evil. As God's people magnify His name and announce His deeds through song, testimony, word and worship, they do battle against the onslaught of Satan and his lies.

Consider once again First Chronicles 15 and 16. David, desiring God's presence in his midst, brings back the Ark of the Covenant during a worship celebration focused upon the glory of God. Could it be that David discerned a critical relationship between declaring God's glory and his own effectiveness as Israel's leader? Did God instruct David to focus upon His glory in order to weaken the power of the evil one and position David for both growth and victory? Is there a relationship between church growth and a congregation intentionally declaring the glory of God in worship? To each question there is ample support to resoundingly say "Yes!"

If churches hope to see people grow in their love for God, receive His wholeness, recognize and realize full potential as

His people—if they want to see the broken made whole and the wounded healed—then they must declare the glory of God in corporate worship. By doing this, worshipers advance the purposes of God's mighty kingdom while frustrating the purposes of Satan who seeks to keep all eyes away from the glory of the Father. When a congregation designs worship services that aggressively glorify God, they are often engaging in spiritual warfare, opening the way to a dynamic unveiling of God's power and presence. And when this happens, both people and churches grow.

Discussion Questions
1. What do you do to encourage sincerity in worship?
2. Allen and Borror state that "worship is not primarily a state of the art but rather a state of the heart." What does this mean?
3. Do worshipers have opportunity for confession in your worship services?
4. How can laypeople prepare Saturday night for Sunday worship? What strategy should be developed for addressing this issue in your church?
5. What can you do to enhance Spirit-filled worship?
6. List several ways worshipers can quench the Spirit. Grieve the Spirit.

CHAPTER

4

Will This Worship Service Be Christ-centered?

W HAT WAS MISSING IN THIS morning's worship service? Driving home, I kept asking myself that question. In general, the service was sound. The pastor preached an excellent sermon from the Old Testament on the sovereignty of God. Whoever organized the service coordinated the hymns and special music around that theme. What was said and sung was straight from Scripture and relevant to daily living. The entire experience was creative and upbeat. But still, something was missing. In some way, the worship service was incomplete.

At home I shared these feelings with my wife, Cheryl, and it did not surprise me when she said she had had the same reaction. She, too, felt an imbalance, an inadequacy. Together we asked ourselves what was missing. Why were we sensing that the service was unfinished? Was there, in fact, a problem with the order of worship, or was the problem in us? The service was solid, but it was not enough.

Suddenly, almost simultaneously, we both realized what was missing. The worship service lacked any intentional reference to the person and work of Jesus Christ. I know the pastor recognized the centrality of Jesus to the Christian faith. The congregation was growing because of an aggressive evangelism program. So a basic love for Jesus was not in question. The problem was one of oversight. But what a disastrous oversight! The worship service did not celebrate Jesus Christ.

Since that time, I have been more attentive to the matter of Christ-centered worship. Unfortunately, I have found that the imbalance occurs too frequently in evangelical worship services. Pastors often build the worship theme around their sermon text. And the problem is that not all texts relate directly to Christ Jesus. When songs, special music, calls to worship and Scripture are chosen to support the general theme and the theme is not gospel-oriented, these forms of worship can and often do omit direct reference to our Lord. If He is not intentionally addressed, a person can go through an entire service without any mention of Jesus our Lord. One may sing and hear of the mighty power of the Father God. But if the worship service fails to focus on Christ, it is inadequate and incomplete.

Certainly worship must glorify the Father. We have already addressed this at length. But balanced worship must also be Christ-centered. Every service, regardless of theme and text, must intentionally highlight the person and work of Jesus. He is at the heart of everything it means to be a Christian. His work is central to the Christian faith. Nowhere is that centrality more important than in our worship services. Christian worship is a celebration of Jesus Christ—God the Son, our living Redeemer. There is no legitimacy to meeting as worshipers if we do not lift Him up.

Be assured that this is not to say *every* sermon, *every* song, *every* creed must focus exclusively on the gospel message. There is not only room, but a need for sermons and songs that deal with other theological issues. But in one form or another, every worship service *must* focus on Jesus Christ.

After all, Jesus has provided our only access to the Father. Without Him, worship is unacceptable and worshipers undeserving. Through Him, believers are called sons and daughters, members of God's eternal kingdom. What we are as God's people and what we offer Him in life and worship is centered in Jesus Christ. In his first epistle, Peter clarifies our Christ-centeredness.

> As you come to him, the living Stone—rejected by men but chosen by God and precious to him—you also, like living stones, are being built into a spiritual house to be a holy priesthood, offering spiritual sacrifices acceptable to God *through Jesus Christ* [italics mine]. (1 Peter 2:4–5)

Worship services must be designed to intentionally highlight the person and work of Jesus Christ. Believers must, in fact, gather to "lift Jesus higher, lift Him up for the world to see." Of course, recognizing this focus is not enough. Leaders must go beyond recognition to actually designing services faithful to this concern. I have found four ingredients of Christ-centered, dynamic worship. As a memory aid, I have labeled them Retell, Remember, Rejoice and Respond.

Retell

In recent years I have become a member of The Christian and Missionary Alliance. Since its beginning, this fast-growing denomination has placed heavy emphasis on evangelism and world missions. For more than 100 years, its members have spanned the globe, spreading the message of new life in Jesus Christ. It is precisely this emphasis that attracted me—and countless others—to the Alliance. The gospel of Christ is at the heart of its ministry and mission.

A.B. Simpson, founder of The Christian and Missionary Alliance, prioritized Jesus in his life and ministry. This focus was reflected in the earliest doctrinal standards of the movement. The central emphasis of Alliance theology was and still is the fourfold gospel: Christ as Savior, Sanctifier, Healer and Coming King. Everything the Alliance believes and does is linked to Jesus—His person and work. I believe this focus is not only valid for the Alliance but for every Christian disciple. The gospel of Jesus is central to our faith.

The gospel of Christ, therefore, must be central to worship. Each service should declare the glorious message of Christ's life, death and resurrection. Songs, sermons, creeds and confessions should retell the story of Jesus. He is the focal point of our celebration and proclamation.

Robert Webber best handles this issue of retelling the gospel message in our worship services. He supports the idea that true worship must focus upon the victory of Christ over all the forces of Satan. In *Worship Is a Verb*, Webber writes,

> I have attended many evangelical worship services in which the underlying drama of Christ's work has not been central and clear. I have longed to hear the words "Christ has overcome all the powers of evil. Be at peace." But this message, the very central proclamation of the faith, is frequently missing. Often the service tells me what I have to do, rather than celebrating what Christ has done. I'm told to live right, to witness, to get myself together, to forgive my enemies, and to give more money. But that's only part of the story. I also need to hear and experience the triumphant note that God has put away evil through his work in Christ. This is the

word that gives me the peace of the Lord and stimulates me to offer my life in the service of Christ.[16]

Worshipers need to rehear the gospel of Jesus Christ. It is the obligation of worship leaders to structure services that retell this good news. Again and again, believers must hear the message that we were lost, broken and dead in sin, but through the life, death and resurrection of Jesus Christ, we are able to receive cleansing, forgiveness, adoption, victory and eternal life in union with God the Father.

It is amazing, but believers never tire of that simple gospel message. We never grow so sophisticated that the good news of Jesus and His redeeming love does not cause a stir deep within. For several years, I was involved in an evangelistic youth camp in western Pennsylvania. For one week, teenagers from the surrounding area gathered for fun, games and, most important, exposure to the gospel of Christ.

How well I remember Jim, a rowdy, rebellious teen who seemed determined to disrupt. His antics frustrated counselors and campers alike. Several counselors even felt it would be best to send him home. But it was just this kind of young person who needed Jesus the most. And unknown to us, everything said about Christ was getting through to Jim loud and clear. The day before camp was to end, this young rebel was revolutionized by a genuine encounter with Christ. The change was radical and obvious to everyone. What a tremendous reminder for all of us of the power of our Redeeming Lord!

Traditionally, the last evening of camp was reserved for a lengthy, yet exciting, worship service. One part of the service was designed to give campers an opportunity to express words of praise. Several students stood and shared how meaningful the experience had been for them. Then Jim stood to his feet, and a silence filled the chapel. He stood for several moments, struggling to hold back tears. Three times he tried to speak, getting out only the name of Jesus before he would choke with emotion. Finally, the fourth time, he began slowly. "Jesus," he said, pausing, again fighting the tears. "Jesus. Friends that's all I can say, but that says it all." And, in fact, his "testimony" did say it all. Jim was lifting up, by his own life experience, the glorious and victorious work of Jesus Christ. That testimony stirred every worshiper present to celebrate the Christ-event.

So it must be in every worship service. Carefully and prayerfully, forms of worship should retell the story of Jesus. While the specific theme of sermons varies, the center of worship is still Jesus Christ. While there are various ways to accomplish this, let us consider four common forms that can readily retell the gospel.

1. *There is the sermon.* Pastors should regularly preach clear gospel messages. Not only is this a key to evangelism, it also keeps believers focused on the work of Christ. A series through a Gospel, on the life and teachings of Jesus, is a must to balanced preaching. Raymond Bryan Brown encourages preachers to guard against imbalanced preaching by following what he calls a "biblical year." He suggests the following calendar:

1. Season of revelation in the Old Testament
   September, October, November
   Emphasis on patriarchs, Moses, prophets, creation, providence, covenant, etc.
2. Season of preparation for the Advent
   December
   Emphasis on Old Testament prophecies, John the Baptist, the "fullness of time"

3. Season of the life and teachings of Christ
   January, February
   Emphasis on great events—the Sermon on the Mount, Jesus' parables, miracles, healings, etc.
4. Season of preparation for Easter
   March
   Emphasis on self-examination, repentance, prayer, reconciliation, renewal, the cross
5. Season of Easter
   April, May
   Emphasis on the risen Christ and the cosmic Christ in Acts and the Letters
6. Season of Pentecost
   June
   Emphasis on the Holy Spirit and the inner life translated into outer witness
7. Season of the life and deeds of the church
   June, July, August
   Emphasis on the doctrine of the church—fellowship, ordinances, beliefs, etc.—and practical application of faith to the problems of everyday life[17]

You will note that Brown's "biblical year" focuses nearly six months on the dynamics of the Christ-event.

2. *The use of creeds keeps worship Christo-centric.* Since the middle of the second century, Christians have recited creeds in worship as a way of rehearsing the gospel. Consider the Apostles' Creed and its glorious retelling of the Christ-event:

I believe in God, the Father Almighty, Maker of heaven and earth; and in Jesus Christ, His only Son our Lord; who was conceived by the Holy Spirit, born of the Virgin Mary, suffered under Pontius Pilate, was crucified, dead, and buried; the third day He rose from the dead; He ascended into heaven, and sitteth at the right hand of God the Father Almighty; from thence He shall come to judge the quick and the dead. I believe in the Holy Spirit; the holy catholic Church, the communion of saints; the forgiveness of sins; the resurrection of the body, and the life everlasting. Amen.

For generations, Christians have recited this creed as a means of reaffirming and refocusing their faith in Jesus Christ. More recently Graham Kendrick, a leader in worship renewal from Great Britain, has paraphrased the Apostles' Creed and put it to song. The piece, entitled "We Believe," has become a favorite at our church in California. People enthusiastically sing, even shout, this wonderful affirmation of the Christian faith. As this happens, an explosion of faith and victory occurs, all in the name of Jesus Christ! It is glorious!

3. *Believers have at their disposal countless songs and choruses that focus on the gospel of Christ.* These songs can serve to direct worship to Jesus as well as to declare the message of His all-redeeming love. Worship leaders can easily keep worship Christo-centric through the choice of music. Consider the message and power of "Fairest Lord Jesus," "Jesus, Thou Joy of Loving Hearts," "Jesus Thy Blood and Righteousness," "Nothing But the Blood," and the A.B. Simpson classic, "Jesus Only." The list of titles is almost endless. Add to these the scores of choruses being written about Christ, and worship leaders have an inexhaustible well from which to draw. Christ-centered singing is the standard of the heavenly throng. Consider this song of heaven recorded in Revelation 5:

You are worthy to take the scroll

and to open its seals,
because you were slain,
and with your blood you purchased men for God
from every tribe and language and people and nation.
You have made them to be a kingdom and priests to
serve our God,
and they will reign on the earth. (verses 9 and 10)

Worthy is the Lamb, who was slain,
to receive power and wealth and wisdom and strength
and honor and glory and praise! (verse 12)

To him who sits on the throne and to the Lamb
be praise and honor and glory and power,
for ever and ever! (verse 13)

Since Christ-centered praise is the standard in glory, let us prepare worshipers here for their eternal inheritance!

4. *Personal testimonies play a significant role in Christ-centered worship.* Granted, the practice has been misused so much that most pastors are afraid of it. As soon as the idea is mentioned, negative images of long, sin-centered meanderings come to mind. How well we remember the times when pastors gave opportunity for a few personal testimonies, never to get the service back again. It is true, testimonies can actually disrupt more than focus a worship service.

But with proper planning and guidance, the personal testimony can still enhance Christ-centered worship. I once attended a new church, where the worship leaders regularly used personal testimonies in the worship service. There was a specific place in the order of service for this. Each week one person was asked to share, for three to five minutes, how Christ Jesus changed his or her life. The participants were contacted in advance and received general guidance on how to present their testimonies. The idea is to highlight *His* story through *their* story. I find it refreshing to hear the ageless message that *Jesus saves!*

. This practice accomplishes two things. First, it refocuses our attention upon the Christ-event in worship. Second, visitors hear a clear, basic presentation of the gospel from an average "unpaid" layperson. This tends to validate the gospel message, attracting the listener to the life-changing Christ. Regardless of sermon text and theme, every week the basic gospel is proclaimed—a practice consistent with Christo-centric worship.

Obviously these are but examples of forms of worship that can keep services focused on Christ. In truth, every form has that same potential. It would not be advisable to do the same thing week after week. Nor would a service be balanced if every song and sermon focused solely on the gospel. Yet, without fail, every worship service must retell the glorious message of Christ. And it is the obligation of pastors and leaders to see that worship does just that.

Remember

A young European pastor, of an earlier era, was prepared to preach on a Sunday morning when he looked out upon the congregation and was shocked to see that the king had come to worship. He immediately set aside his sermon and proceeded to praise the king for his leadership, wisdom and benevolence. The next week the young pastor received a gift from the king. It was a beautiful wooden cross. The king asked that this cross be hung where the preacher could easily see it, so that he would be reminded of the *true* focal point of the worship experience—the cross!

The Christ-event is central to our faith, and central to the

Christ-event is the cross. It was at Calvary, nearly 2,000 years ago, that Jesus reconciled humankind to God. At the unbelievable price of His shed blood and broken body, believers receive cleansing and redemption. It is Christ's atoning sacrifice that sets people free from death, giving victory and life everlasting to those who believe. We must never forget the centrality of His sacrificial death. The Lord calls us to continually remember His death until He returns to take the church into God's eternal glory!

It is far too easy to underemphasize the place of the cross in our faith. The "name it and claim it" cults place an emphasis on success and abundance. They treat suffering as sin and focus more on receiving than giving. It is difficult to reconcile the cross to such a theology, so they often overlook or underemphasize it.

In addition, churches can fail to balance the victory of Christ's resurrection with the sufferings of Calvary. True, each Sunday must be a celebration of the Living Lord. But we must balance our celebration with solemnity. As we rejoice in resurrection power, we must not forget the atoning death of Christ on Calvary. His death is the grand prelude to the Easter announcement.

Christo-centric worship calls us to remember Christ's atoning work by regularly celebrating the Lord's Supper. Instituted by our Lord, Communion calls the church back to Calvary. Jesus shared broken bread with His disciples, a symbol of His broken body. He then shared the cup, signifying His shed blood. Since then, the church has repeated this practice as a way of calling the Lord's followers back to the cross. While varying in form and frequency, celebrating the Lord's Supper has been basic to the church down through the ages. It is an integral part of balanced Christian worship.

The Lord's Supper can and should be a powerful event in

the worship service. But only careful planning can keep it meaningful and fresh. Although churches should observe Communion regularly, it must not become a liturgical form devoid of life. Leaders must work hard at this, or else the practice will become predictable, or even worse, habitual. Communion is *not* an end in itself. Rather it is an act that should cause us to remember the sacrificial death of the Lord Jesus. More than that, at the table of Communion, we experience and celebrate the very presence of the Savior.

1. *The Lord's Supper calls the church to remember what is behind.* It is a look back to Calvary. In First Corinthians, the Apostle Paul views the Lord's Supper as an act of worship. He writes:

> For I received from the Lord what I also passed on to you: The Lord Jesus, on the night he was betrayed, took bread, and when he had given thanks, he broke it and said, "This is my body, which is for you; do this in remembrance of me." In the same way, after supper he took the cup, saying, "This cup is the new covenant in my blood; do this whenever you drink it, in remembrance of me." For whenever you eat this bread and drink this cup, you proclaim the Lord's death until he comes. (11:23–26)

For centuries, the Israelites marked and remembered the Exodus with the Feast of Passover. It was a memorial celebration, calling people back to their deliverance from slavery. Likewise, the Lord's Supper is a memorial feast that calls Christians to remember. Each time we share that meal, we look back to Calvary through the symbolic portrayal of Christ's death on the cross.

2. *Celebrating the Lord's Supper in worship also calls the*

church to remember what is ahead. In Matthew's Gospel we read,

> While they were eating, Jesus took bread, gave thanks and broke it, and gave it to his disciples, saying, "Take and eat; this is my body."
>
> Then he took the cup, gave thanks and offered it to them, saying, "Drink from it, all of you. This is my blood of the covenant, which is poured out for many for the forgiveness of sins. I tell you, I will not drink of this fruit of the vine from now on until that day when I drink it anew with you in my Father's kingdom." (26:26–29)

Note how the Lord brings the future and past together in this one event. While calling His disciples to remember His atoning death, He sets before them the hope of the kingdom. He puts suffering in perspective. Someday, because of Calvary, we will sit down with Christ and feast in the kingdom of God. The suffering of this age is brought into focus by the hope of eternal glory. Paul echoes this future glance in the Communion celebration, calling it a proclamation of the Lord's death until He comes. Thus, Christ-centered worship, through the Lord's Supper, calls us to remember what was and what is to come in Christ Jesus.

3. *Remembrance of the Lord's death also calls us to look beyond the church to the lost world.* The message of the Lord's Supper is one of redemption. The Lord Jesus was broken in order to reconcile the lost to God. As His body, the church is to carry on that ministry of reconciliation. Wheat and grapes must be crushed before they become the nourishment of bread and wine. Jesus was broken to bring life to

all who believe. In turn, the church must sacrifice and carry the cross as part of its ministry to a dark world.

4. *The Lord's Supper calls us to remember the sacrificial nature of our servanthood.* Christianity is not all blessings and victory celebration. Faith involves surrender, suffering and also selflessness. I need that reminder. So do most Christians. Christian disciples are reminded that self-centeredness is unacceptable. Like Jesus, the church must be willing to be broken so that the battered, darkened world may be saved.

The Lord's Supper calls us to remember. It is a memorial feast that reminds the church of what is behind us—the cross; what is ahead—the kingdom; and what is all about us—an unreconciled world for which Christ died. Such a reminder should be central to our worship experience. These truths are integral to everything it means to be a Christian.

5. *The Lord's Supper spiritually unites the redeemed with their Redeemer.* There is an unquestionable, yet mystical dynamic that occurs as Christians celebrate the Eucharist. While remembering the past work of the Lord, believers experience Christ afresh, present through the Holy Spirit. If open to His presence, congregations can be unusually and wonderfully touched by His power. Believing this, Risen King Community Church encourages people to receive special prayer for personal needs during the service of Communion. As a result countless people have received freedom from bondage, healing both spiritual and emotional, and salvation, all while the body gathers at the Table of the Lord. The point is simply this: Jesus Christ is present with us in the celebration of His death. Expect to meet Him there!

Practically, each local church must decide how frequently it will observe the Lord's Supper. Traditions vary from denomination to denomination and church to church. Pastors and leaders must work hard to keep the practice fresh and full of meaning. Great care and prayer should precede each participation. Identifying the different ways congregations celebrate the Lord's Supper can help. Variety and creativity enhance the meaning and message of this cornerstone ordinance of our Christian faith. Whatever we do, let us remember this cross-centered focus of our corporate worship services.

Rejoice

Is your worship service a celebration? It certainly should be! Christian worship is intricately rooted in that first Lord's day celebration, when the announcement came that Jesus had risen from the dead.

Disheartened and disillusioned, Jesus' disciples had watched their Lord die on Calvary. For them, hopes and dreams were dashed. Their Messiah was dead, savagely crucified as a common criminal. Imagine the emptiness, the agony, the despair they must have felt! All their tomorrows seemed to die with Jesus.

But out of the darkness came a great and shining light. On that early Sunday morning, the first Christian worship service began. And the theme was not death but life! Jesus broke the chains of darkness and rose from the grave with resurrection power—victor over the dark domain! Sadness was turned to eternal joy. The disciples, full of emotion, celebrated Jesus, the risen, living Lord. Who could ever adequately describe their excitement and unimaginable rejoicing?

The spirit of celebration that characterized that first worship service should be evident every time we gather to praise His name. Christian worship is a celebration, an Easter morning celebration every week of the year. Believers should gather with hearts full of praise, declaring with those first disciples: *Jesus Lives!*

Achieving this celebration spirit, however, is not easy. Worship leaders have to work hard at it. Retelling and remembering should lead to great rejoicing, but that does not always happen. I believe there is little worse than celebrating the Lord of resurrection power in a funereal atmosphere. Worship absent of celebration and rejoicing violates the very truth we proclaim. Soon people believe the mood and reject the message of new life.

When I was a small boy, my family did not attend church regularly. But occasionally my mother would take my sister and me to midweek services. How well I remember one particular Wednesday night. Few people attended the service. The singing seemed lifeless, the prayers long and the message very, very dry. I am not sure the topic was eternity, but it seemed that the service was going on for ever and ever. To be honest, I was thoroughly bored.

Finally the last hymn was sung. Soon I could go home— even homework would be more interesting! Suddenly the pastor stopped between stanzas, making some comments on how great it was to praise God together. I was not impressed or moved. That is, until he said the following: "And just think, this is what heaven is going to be like!" That night the pastor left an impression on me that he never intended. If heaven was to be like that service, I had just lost all interest in going there. Quite frankly, the church was a long time in regaining my attention!

True Christian worship is far from boring and lifeless. It is a dynamic celebration of the Living Lord of resurrection power. There is a spirit of excitement and rejoicing that is electrifying. Far from "cold and frozen," Christ-centered worshipers are full of life, anxious to declare the praises of their reigning King.

Pastors and leaders must design worship services that reflect just that image. We should bring into our celebrations sights and sounds that create an atmosphere of life. Here are some ways to do that.

1. *Sing positive, uplifting and enthusiastic songs.* "He Lives" is one that always excites me.

> I serve a risen Saviour, He's in the world today;
> I know that He is living, whatever men may say;
> I see His hand of mercy, I hear His voice of cheer;
> And just the time I need Him, He's always near.
> Rejoice, rejoice, O Christian, lift up your voice and sing
> Eternal hallelujahs to Jesus Christ the King!
> The hope of all who seek Him, the help of all who find,
> None other is so loving, so good and kind.
> He lives, He lives, Christ Jesus lives today,
> He walks with me and talks with me,
> Along life's narrow way.
> He lives, He lives, salvation to impart,
> You ask me how I know He lives? He lives within my
>   heart.

These are words that generate life in worship, because they point to the glorious Lord of life.

2. *Use praises and testimonies to create a deep sense of joy and celebration in worship.* Worshipers need to hear of Christ's victories in the lives of others. As another Christian stands and shares about the Lord's provision, he or she encourages others to trust in the Lord of life. Such positive words bring hope and joy to troubled hearts. That should be standard fare in Christ-centered worship.

3. *Employ color and movement in your celebrations.* Creative banners, hung in the sanctuary, can illustrate themes of life, hope and joy. Every legitimate art form is employed to create an atmosphere of rejoicing. Worship becomes a celebration, as it should be.

Obviously, the practical implementation of such forms of Christ-centered worship takes careful planning. To be sure, some congregations would need to move slowly. Too much too soon, could intimidate the more reserved worshipers.

It is critical to remember that what is acceptable in one culture may be inappropriate in another. To some, celebration includes tambourines and guitars. To others, the use of such instruments would be inappropriate, even offensive. Be careful not to impose forms of worship and celebration upon your congregation. Forms must fit the context, moving people to rejoice in Christ in terms familiar to their day-to-day practices. From there, over time, leaders can move worshipers to new experiences and expressions of Christ-centered praise.

Finally, just a reminder that celebration and solemnity are to be in balance. This we discussed at some length previously. The spirit of rejoicing in Christian worship cannot be shallow. It is rooted in retelling and remembering the glorious gospel of Christ's life, death and resurrection. There must be depth to the message if the celebration is to have meaning. And there is no deeper message than that of Christ's all-redeeming love. Christ-centered worship is characterized by rejoicing because it is rooted in the greatest message humanity has ever heard—Jesus lives!

Respond

Consider the birth narrative of our Lord Jesus. Christ came to deliver humanity from sin and brokenness. He was proclaimed by angel messengers as the Son of David and Savior of mankind. The glorious celebration was amplified by an angel choir singing "Glory to God on High." The greatest message ever heard was proclaimed through the region. Christ Jesus, Savior of the world was born. And every person listed in the narrative responded to the announcement of His birth.

To Herod, this message was a threat to his own kingdom. His response was one of rejection. To the innkeeper, his life was too busy for such an untimely intrusion. His response was one of apathy. For others, such as the shepherds and the magi, this message of salvation was welcome; the Child was worthy of worship and dedication. Regardless of the type of response, everyone touched by the Christ-event did respond.

As it was, so it shall be. Wherever and whenever the message of Christ is celebrated or proclaimed, there is need for response. People will be moved to act as we lift Jesus higher in worship. Pastors and worship leaders must recognize this dynamic of Christ-centered worship and design services accordingly. Worshipers are confronted with the gospel of Christ, not just to present information to them but so that they might answer His life-changing invitation. Providing opportunity for response completes the action of true Christ-centered worship. Services lacking opportunity for a response are unfinished, incomplete. Response is the natural and expected reaction to any encounter with God.

Isaiah 6 outlines a pattern of worship that models the interrelationship of praise, proclamation and response. Isaiah's vision begins at the throne of God, where he sees the Lord high and lifted up. Praise and adoration characterize the activity before the Almighty, as the prophet hears the heavenly host declare,

> Holy, holy, holy is the LORD Almighty;
>   the whole earth is full of his glory. (verse 3)

Isaiah's response is to confess. Having seen the glory of the Lord, he is now sickened by his own depravity and declares,

> Woe to me! . . . I am ruined! For I am a man of unclean lips, and I live among a people of unclean lips, and my eyes have seen the King, the LORD Almighty. (verse 5)

The Lord then sends a seraph to Isaiah. He takes a live coal from the altar and touches the prophet's mouth. The angel declares the Word of the Lord,

> Your guilt is taken away and your sin atoned for. (verse 7)

This is followed by God's call to Isaiah,

> Whom shall I send? And who will go for us? (verse 8)

Again Isaiah responds. Having been cleansed by Almighty God and his sin atoned for, Isaiah declares, "Here am I. Send me!" (verse 8).

It is easy to see a pattern in this divine encounter—an order to the worship.

Praise—The Lord is high and lifted up.
Response—Isaiah, overwhelmed in God's presence, confesses his own depravity.
Ministry of the Word—The Lord declares both forgiveness and a call to service.

Response—Spontaneously, having been touched by the Lord, and having heard His Word, the prophet volunteers, "Send me!"

I found this model helpful in designing worship services. We began each service with high praise, lifting before the Lord songs and words of adoration. This was followed by a response of confession. Sensing and declaring the glory of God in turn revealed our own sin. Before moving on in worship, this sin had to be confessed and cleansed. Whether corporately or personally, the worshipers had opportunity to pour out their hearts before the Lord. Not only is confession the natural response of praise, it is the critical preparation for hearing the Word of the Lord.

Next came the proclamation of the Word. I moved Scripture reading and preaching from the end of the service to the middle. Not only did this help change the perception that the sermon was the highlight and climax of the service, it also provided ample time for response. Following the sermon, worshipers were given opportunity to acknowledge God's presence and obey His Word. This response time included altar prayer, songs of dedication, testimonies and praises. The service concluded with the offering (symbolic of the offering of our lives) and doxology. Together, the congregation responded with thanks for all God's blessings as the final act of corporate worship. While the forms of worship can vary from week to week, such a basic outline keeps the service balanced and provides valid opportunities for response. (An outline of this particular order of worship is included in Appendix B.)

It is important to address the issue of manipulation as it relates to congregational response. Pastors, myself included, have a strong desire to see results. This desire, if unchecked, can lead to manipulation, forcing people to unnaturally respond to a message or other form of worship.

I experienced a classic example of this at a camp meeting. Following the evangelist's sermon, there was an appeal for response. First, he asked interested people to pray to receive Christ. Then he appealed to those who prayed to raise their hands, followed by a request that they stand and then come forward.

I could sense the tension. People were being manipulated. They did not know that their initial prayer would require a public response at a camp meeting altar. The evangelist should have made the demands clear before he asked people to pray. In this case few responded to the appeal. This led the speaker to broaden the invitation. He asked people to come who had prayed to receive Christ, then also those concerned about a loved one, followed by an appeal to anyone with a need in his or her life who wanted prayer. His desire for visual response was inappropriate.

Response in worship must be natural and spontaneous. Leaders should provide opportunity, yet never push people with any type of hard sell. Worship services should be designed with response in mind. Times of confession, prayer, praise and offering are not only appropriate, they are necessary. But let the Spirit lead the worshiper to participate. If God is truly lifted up, if Christ is clearly proclaimed, people will act. When God moves, we simply need to open the door—and open the door we must.

What happens when worshipers are not given the chance to respond? First, if they cannot respond with a time of confession, it becomes difficult to move on in worship. Praise may have identified their problem areas, but identification is not enough. Worshipers need a time of emptying in order to be filled with God's Word and Spirit. Second, if we fail to give opportunity for response after hearing the Word, worshipers may not embrace or digest the truth.

Before I rearranged the worship service in the church I pastored, people often experienced frustration. They would hear the Word; it would convince and convict, but within minutes of the conclusion, they were out of the church and driving home. The truth quickly faded from their minds.

I soon learned that there must be time to work the Word into the heart. Again, that time is structured, yet an open opportunity for response. When Christ is proclaimed and His presence felt, to respond is the only acceptable thing we can do.

Discussion Questions

1. Review your last four worship services. How would you evaluate their Christ-centeredness?
2. Make a list of songs, sermons, creeds and testimonies in those services that directly pointed to Christ.
3. Survey your hymnal. What songs can you list that clearly retell the message of Christ?
4. Briefly write your testimony. Include the following three basic elements:
   a. in general terms, what life was like before you became a Christian;
   b. how you came to know Christ;
   c. what life has been like since conversion.
   Do this on no more than one sheet of paper, then share it with your discussion group.
5. Where would testimonies best fit into your worship service? What safeguards would you need to insure that they complemented the service?
6. What traditions does your church follow regarding the Lord's Supper? How frequently is it included in worship?

7. List ways you could vary the practice of Communion to keep it fresh and meaningful. You may want to contact several churches to see how they include the Lord's Supper in their worship.

8. What ingredients do you feel are critical to creating an atmosphere of celebration and rejoicing in worship?

9. How would worshipers in your local church respond to celebration banners? If positively, can you think of people gifted to make them? What themes would you want to portray?

10. Review your last four worship services again. Where and in what way were worshipers encouraged to respond to God's presence and His Word?

11. Can you think of any changes needed in the order of worship that would better encourage response?

Will This Worship Service Edify Believers?

O N THE LAST SUNDAY of each year, Pastor Stevens would begin his sermon with the same question. People in the congregation heard it year after year, yet never tired of the inquiry. In fact, that Sunday became a favorite, precisely because of this yearly tradition. The question was certainly predictable, but it never grew old. It was one of the most relevant questions asked of them, a sort of checkpoint for their spiritual pilgrimage. As faithful as the changing year, Pastor Stevens would say, "Beloved, another year is almost gone. Have you become more like Jesus?"

With that single question, the pastor identified the main goal of Christian discipleship—becoming more like Jesus. Day by day, month by month and year after year, followers of Christ are to change. This movement toward Christlikeness is a primary characteristic of spiritual health and maturity. It is the standard of true biblical faith. Christians are never to stay the same; they should never stagnate. They are to be built up in the Lord Jesus.

As we all know, the local church is to play a crucial role in edifying believers. Pastors, evangelists and teachers are called to lead men and women to spiritual maturity. Paul spoke of this in both Colossians 2 and Ephesians 4.

> So then, just as you received Christ Jesus as Lord, continue to live in him, rooted and built up in him, strengthened in the faith as you were taught, and overflowing with thankfulness. (Colossians 2:6,7)

> It was he [Jesus] who gave some to be apostles, some to be prophets, some to be evangelists, and some to be pastors and teachers, to prepare God's people for works of service, so that the body of Christ may be built up until we all reach unity in the faith and in the knowledge of the Son of God and become mature, attaining to the whole measure of the fullness of Christ. (Ephesians 4:11–13)

Paul's admonition is clear. One aspect of Christian ministry is edification—building people up in Christ.

Local church leaders should be concerned about the spiritual development of their people. Christians need regular nourishment and teaching from the Word of God. By example and instruction, pastors must set before their flocks the standard of Christian faith, character and conduct. Without this, Christians grow weak. They struggle with immaturity, often compromising their discipleship with un-Christian attitudes and actions. When not led otherwise, whole congregations can evidence a kind of spiritual malnutrition. Peter Wagner identifies this problem as a church growth disease called Arrested Spiritual Development. People are simply not becoming more like Jesus.

Pastors and church leaders must use every ministry-mode

available to present people mature in Christ. Preaching, teaching, discipling, counseling and prayer each become the tools for building believers. Just as a contractor constructs a building piece by piece, so ministers are to raise up strong disciples. Lesson by lesson, they teach the basic principles of life and godliness. As men and women integrate the lessons of faith into their lives, they become stronger. Soon pastors can see a new spiritual vitality and maturity in the congregation. Instead of ministering to spiritual infants, pastors are helping people attain the full measure of Christ.

When setting goals and implementing programs for spiritual development, leaders should take careful note of the worship service. It is an important resource for the edification of believers. As people gather to worship, both the presence of God and the proclamation of His Word call them to change. Yes, worship is primarily focused upon God. Yet, services can and should include challenges directed to the worshiper. Sermons, songs, testimonies and prayers can call people to Christlikeness. This principle of worship must be recognized and developed by church leaders.

While every pastor would love to have all of his people in Christian education classes and Bible studies, such is not the case. Only a percentage of people in every congregation get involved in these direct teaching and training programs. For many, the only involvement in the local church is through the worship service. It becomes the pastor's sole opportunity to build brick upon brick. As such, worship becomes a natural and necessary opportunity for edifying—an opportunity we cannot afford to miss.

Pastors and church leaders should carefully and intentionally plan each service with this goal in mind. Services must not only glorify God and be Christ-centered, they must also edify believers. A basic commitment to this principle can be readily translated into regular practice by following four imperatives: inspire, instruct, involve and integrate. Designing services faithful to these principles will help worshipers become more like Jesus.

Inspire

I shall never forget my first visit to the Crystal Cathedral. I was studying church growth at Fuller Theological Seminary. While there, I wanted to develop case studies on some of the mega-churches in southern California. As far as I was concerned, Garden Grove was the place to start. A dynamic, fast-growing congregation, the Crystal Cathedral should be an important church for me to observe. It was. Some of the key lessons I learned came from the Sunday morning worship service.

I was somewhat overwhelmed by the size and beauty of the building as I sat and waited for the service to begin. To that point, everything I saw and experienced had been impressive. There was easy access to parking, clear directions to the sanctuary, warm greetings and help from ushers and an unusual friendliness from members of the church. Everything was positive and a tremendous example for any student of church growth. But as the saying goes, "I hadn't seen anything yet!" Suddenly, almost unexpectedly, I was ushered into one of the most inspiring worship services I had ever experienced.

It is difficult to express what I saw, heard and felt at the beginning of the service. As I said previously, I was sitting in the auditorium taking in the building's beauty when suddenly my attention was drawn to the front. The organist began playing, and the organ's notes silenced the gathering crowd, drawing it into worship. At the same time, trumpets sent a blast of sound across the auditorium, while fountains, built down the middle of the main floor, sent streams of water reaching for the ceiling. Sound and movement filled those first moments of the service, creating a sense of excitement and expectation. I felt as if something wonderful was about to happen.

In the midst of this concert of sight and sound, the entire right wall of glass began to open. The outside world was ushered into this glorious pageantry of praise. Dr. Schuller appeared, slowly walking the length of the stage toward the opening wall. Suddenly, the auditorium became silent. Dr. Schuller, arms outstretched before God and congregation declared, "This is the day that the Lord has made. Let us rejoice and be glad in it!"

To say the least, I was inspired! My focus was drawn Godward, my heart uplifted and my spirit full of excitement and anticipation. From there we were all led through a positive, upbeat service of worship and praise. Say what you may about Robert Schuller, he knows how to design services that breathe life into people.

Obviously, few can or should duplicate all that happens at the Crystal Cathedral. Certainly all would agree that true worship is more than theatrics and esthetics. Neither are in any way a substitute for the Holy Spirit's presence and power. Yet behind the elaborate services at Schuller's church is a principle—a principle all local churches must, at God's leading, embrace—worship services should be inspiring. Why? Because first we are focusing on the Almighty God of the universe. He is the Creator, the Author of life and the Sustainer of all that is. Worship services should create a sense of wonder and power in people as they come into His presence. Second, worship services should be inspiring because worshipers desperately need new life.

I love how Webster's *New World Dictionary* defines *inspire*: to breathe life! That is precisely what worship services should do—breathe life. Believers come to worship from ministry in the world. They have been knocked around by the enemy, defeated in areas of discipleship and drained from ministering to the battered and broken. They come in need of renewal, refilling and revival of soul and spirit. Designed properly, the worship service can become that place of new life. It should be a place of edification, filling disciples so they can go again into the world—spilling over with Living Water to the thirsty, giving life to the sick and dying.

Worship services should cause people to come alive in their Christian experience. Spirits should be uplifted, as sights and sounds, words and music, affirm the message of Christ as Victor and Redeemer. Believers need not only a cognitive understanding of these themes, but an intuitive, subjective affirmation and response. While some are wary of any display of emotion, we should not run from that part of our humanity. God has made us with emotions. He wants not only to touch our minds but to uplift our spirits as well. I believe He wants believers to engage emotionally in worship, so that He might inspire and refill them. As we have noted, emotion alone is shallow and dangerous. But balanced with strong biblical input and the leading of the Spirit, it is an ingredient of renewal.

Some may be uncomfortable with this "person-directed" appeal in worship. They may call us to remember that true worship is something given to God without concern for the worshiper. I agree that this is the primary focus. Our first goal is to glorify God. We come to extol and praise His Holy name. We must never lose sight of that purpose. With that foremost in our mind, we still have to remember that worship does something to us as worshipers. It affects us through the overflow effect of praise. True praise and proclamation of God's Word inspires people. They become excited about discipleship. As they are cleansed in God's presence, they are filled to overflowing. They leave worship equipped to go out and serve the Lord. Worship leaders must recognize this principle and design services that can freely channel this spirit of life. It is part of edifying, part of presenting people mature in Christ.

Here are several key ingredients that can make worship services inspiring to worshipers.

1. *Inspiring services emphasize positive and victorious themes.* Services must never leave the impression that Christians are a defeated people. Worshipers should hear uplifting reminders that God is sovereign, Christ is victor and we are more than conquerors through Him. Ours is a message of hope, forgiveness, joy and eternal life in Jesus our Lord. These are wonderful, glorious themes that breathe life into people—constant promises that the Lord reigns.

This does not mean pastors should bypass the critical issues of sin and brokenness. Certainly we must identify the root problems of life. But our focus should not be on the ugliness of sin; it should be on the beauty of the Overcomer! The good news is not the gloom of sin, death and hell. It is that Jesus came to save. How desperately people need to hear that message. In a world full of as many problems as ours is, the church must offer hope. It must be a vehicle of renewal and new life.

2. *Music is a key ingredient in the worship service.* It has the power to uplift and encourage. Anointed of God, carefully selected music can open worshipers to the Spirit's touch. Pastors, worship committees and leaders must select songs that emphasize the positive, victorious themes. Yes, there is not only room but need for more solemn, reflective songs

that call people to the cross and repentance. But likewise, selections should be chosen that cause hearts to soar.

3. *Times of praise provide opportunities for inspiration.* Positive words of praise remind worshipers that God is active and intervening in the trials of life. As one believer speaks of the Lord's provision, another is encouraged to trust in Him. One person's praise to God for healing uplifts the spirit of another's hurting heart. Hearing that the Lord forgives causes the sinful person to repent. Such Spirit-led opportunities can be as life-giving as fresh air to the suffocating.

4. *Prayer can inspire and bring hope to the worshiper.* Prayer is primarily Godward, but when audible, it declares a message to all who hear. The high priestly prayer of Jesus in John 17 is a prime example. Though directed to God, it conveyed words of hope, comfort, provision and protection to the disciples. This is equally possible with all corporate prayer. We make a mistake if all we do is go through a litany of needs. That can be depressing, not inspiring. People hear only of illnesses, trials and problems. True corporate prayer includes words of faith and hope. Requests are lifted to God because He can meet all needs. Conveying that spirit in prayer encourages people, and they are filled with life. They are inspired!

The possibilities to inspire in worship go on and on. But life-giving worship services do not just happen. They must be backed with prayer and careful planning. This is the obligation of pastors and worship leaders. This is the opportunity for life-giving worship that edifies believers.

Instruct

Ian Pitt-Watson, professor of preaching and practical theology at Fuller Theological Seminary, has written a book on homiletics entitled *A Primer for Preachers*. In many ways it is a basic text for the beginning preacher. Yet, the volume contains refreshing insights that would benefit even the most seasoned expositor. As one might suspect, Pitt-Watson holds a high view of preaching. In his book, he calls the reader to consider the "shattering power of the Word of God, of the destructive consequences of its misuse, but above all of the revolutionary potential of that Word to change lives and to change our world."[18]

You may remember that in the first chapter I said sermon-centered worship was unbalanced. But do not think I am downplaying the importance of preaching. Like Pitt-Watson, I believe it to be a critical and dynamic ingredient in raising up strong Christians. Through biblical preaching, people encounter the Living God. That encounter is, of course, the ultimate goal of true worship, and it has the potential to transform lives. As men and women hear the Word of God faithfully proclaimed, they are edified, and they become more and more like the Lord Jesus.

God's people not only need His Word, they hunger for it. In recent years, there has been an increased concern among laypeople for Bible teaching and preaching. Remarking on this, Ian Pitt-Watson said:

> I doubt if ever the ability to preach has stood higher in the list of priorities of the average pastor search committee. . . . There is little doubt that ordinary people in our churches are saying loudly and clearly, "Give us more and better preaching."[19]

Few people today will tolerate consistently poor sermons. Find a church where preaching is weak, and you will often find a malnourished congregation, dwindling in size.

Likewise, where there is dynamic worship with strong biblical preaching, exciting things are taking place. People are growing, strengthened to love and serve Him more. Granted, most of us are neither Swindolls nor MacArthurs, yet every pastor is obliged to feed his people nourishing truth from Scripture. This is an essential of the Christian faith and a fundamental part of worship that edifies believers.

What kind of preaching edifies believers?

1. *Foremost, it must be biblical preaching.* When a preacher stands in the pulpit, he is there to do one thing—proclaim the Word of the Lord. This is his singular task. Personal opinion or popular philosophy will be quickly forgotten. Only Scripture will endure in the hearts and minds of people. Only biblical preaching has the power to transform lives. It corrects, rebukes, reproves and instructs. It is the Bible that reveals the gospel, feeds the soul, builds disciples and solves life's problems. The Bible alone gives the preacher authority to speak. Only it brings forth faith and fruit. What is it that builds and instructs in worship? It is the Bible!

2. *Preaching that edifies is systematic.* By this I mean it consistently covers the primary matters of Christian faith and practice. As stated earlier, preaching is a brick-by-brick operation. Each week the pastor seeks to lead his people into deeper truth, building on what has gone before. Such building must be well planned and balanced. Pastors should not avoid certain biblical truths or spend disproportionate amounts of time on others. Preaching that edifies is balanced and well-distributed across the biblical and doctrinal spectrum.

I make three suggestions that you may find helpful. First, develop a preaching cycle similar to that of Raymond Brown (mentioned in chapter 4). Dividing the year in this way will help keep preaching balanced. By doing so, you are sure to declare the whole counsel of God.

Second, regularly preach through entire books of the Bible. Series-preaching is nourishing and instructive. People are able to work through the texts, systematically feeding from individual verses and chapters. Each book is full of inspired truth and relevant to daily living.

Third, consider developing a list of important theological issues and topics. Pastor and noted author David Seamands has "a kerygma list" of 100 theological categories. He tries to cover each of these 100 topics at least once every two years.

These approaches can keep the pastor from preaching either a scattering of unrelated topics or a constant diet of personal preferences.

3. *Preaching that edifies believers must also be doctrinally sound.* Careful exegesis and interpretation must precede sermon construction. Good expository preaching is guided by and limited to the theology of the text itself. When proclaiming a passage of Scripture, the faithful preacher does not superimpose biases upon the texts. He is careful at this point, for it is a principle of hermeneutics commonly violated. Too many preachers declare more personal preference than they do biblical principle. The text becomes simply a springboard for them to launch into their private agendas. People need God's Word, not our opinions.

4. *If believers are to be edified, sermons must have a single focus.* Preachers should not try to tell people two or three different things in the same message. Rather, it is best to say one thing three or four different ways. Obviously, any sermon needs sub-points, illustrations, definitions and the like. But these should all support one clear, identifiable biblical theme. People should leave worship knowing exactly what the message was about.

In my homiletics class, students are taught to state their entire sermon theme in one, clear sentence. Everything else said in the message should point to that central truth. This principle of good preaching is shared by the best expositors. In *Between Two Worlds*, John Stott quotes several authors who emphasize the importance of identifying the text's one main thought. One of these is Charles Simeon. He wrote:

> Reduce your text to a simple proposition, and lay that down as the warp; and then make use of the text itself as the woof; illustrating the main idea by the various terms in which it is contained. Screw the word into the minds of your hearers. *A screw is the strongest of all mechanical powers . . . when it has turned a few times, scarcely any power can pull it out.*[20]

Stott illustrates this point further by referring to J.H. Jowett.

> *I have a conviction that no sermon is ready for preaching . . . until we can express its theme in a short, pregnant sentence as clear as a crystal.* I find the getting of that sentence is the hardest, the most exacting and the most fruitful labour in my study . . . I do not think any sermon ought to be preached, or even written, until that sentence has emerged, clear and lucid as a cloud-less moon.[21]

This practice is fundamental to preaching that would truly edify God's people.

5. *Proper use of illustrations can literally make or break a sermon.* In today's world, sermons packed with detail and information just do not communicate. Despite our high-tech age, listening skills may be at an all-time low. The

average attention span is limited, almost defying capture by a 20- to 30-minute sermon. Because of this reality, illustration has become an indispensable ingredient in good preaching.

Not only are illustrations attention-grabbers, they shed light on the theme being proclaimed. The late Clarence MacCartney, noted Presbyterian preacher, said, "Sermons need windows so light can stream in and illumine the abstract interior." Pastor Edward Marquart has coined the acronym SAI, representing stories, analogies and images. In respect to using SAIs as illustrations, Marquart says,

> SAIs are like windows of a house; they bring light, freshness and a pleasure to a sermon. A persistent theme echoed by all authors we are surveying is the power of SAIs to move, change and transform a person. Reason appeals primarily to the mind. SAIs appeal both to the mind and the emotions. As someone said, "Reason assaults the fortress walls of the mind, but stories slip gently through the back door into the heart . . . and begin to change us." [22]

The creative preacher can find illustrations everywhere—personal experience, observation, reading. A careful search yields illustrations that can be vivid and memorable. They are great tools for teaching and a great help in keeping the message fresh and full of life. Try to season sermons with a generous supply of illustrations. They will be, as one author has said, "the raisins in the oatmeal."

6. *Be sure that sermons have a clear purpose and application.* Unlike lectures, sermons are not meant to simply convey information about biblical history. Sermons do more—they seek change on the part of the listener. God's Word calls for

a personal response. When the preacher stands in the pulpit, he should have a clear purpose in mind. What change or action should take place in the life of the hearer? Jay Adams has written a helpful book on this topic. In it he says,

> I am convinced that purpose is of such vital importance to all a preacher does that it ought to control his thinking and actions from start to finish in the preparation and delivery of sermons.[23]

Hoping to further emphasize this point, Adams adds:

> This matter of purpose is such an important consideration in preaching that if your wife were to awaken you on Sunday morning at 4 o'clock and ask, "What is the purpose of this morning's message?" you ought to be able to rattle it off in one crisp sentence, roll over and go to sleep again, all without missing a single stroke in your snoring![24]

The effective preacher not only recognizes the importance of purpose, but identifies the desired response of each sermon. Is it to persuade, encourage, strengthen, inspire or challenge?

Application in preaching helps the listener to fulfill the purpose of the text. This is where the truth of the Word is integrated into the daily life of the believer. Application moves people to action. Without this the preacher has done little more than inform. And quite frankly, most congregations are overinformed. They have so much information that they do not know what to do with it. Good preaching informs less and applies more. People are called to a divine encounter, where the claims of Scripture demand a life-changing response. Expositors may vary on the types and placement of applications. But they are united on this one point: "A sermon rises or falls in its application."[25]

7. *Preaching that edifies is characterized by passion.* Passion, according to the dictionary, "usually implies a strong emotion that has an overpowering or compelling effect." This is precisely the qualifying mark of effective, dynamic preaching. Several ingredients are at work in the man who declares God's Word with passion. First, he has personally encountered the truth of the text being proclaimed. Far from being an objective observer, the preacher has wrestled with the implications of the passage in his own life. He comes into the presence of men and women after having been transformed by his own interaction with God's Word.

Second, he is moved by the urgency of the hour. The 17th-century pietist Richard Baxter said it best when he declared that he preached as a dying man to dying men. For many in your congregation, eternal issues hang in the balance. An unemotional stance is not only unacceptable, it is sinful.

Third, the impassioned preacher is anointed by God's Spirit. Saturated with prayer, the effective messenger speaks with a power from above. This spiritual touch sets the preacher ablaze with a fire that can reach in and touch even the coldest of hearts.

Obviously, these brief comments in no way exhaust this matter of effective preaching. I do hope, however, that they serve as a motivator for pastors seeking to edify believers through the sermon. People desperately need to be instructed in the Word of God. Every worship service offers a tremendous opportunity to do just that.

Involve

I love to worship with the people of Cedar Boulevard

Neighborhood Church, a congregation of The Christian and Missionary Alliance located in Newark, California. Senior pastor, Floyd Evers, and executive pastor, Carl Medford, believe in the power of dynamic worship. One of the key ingredients in their services is congregational involvement. At CBNC worship is not a spectator sport. It calls for the total participation of everyone in attendance. Unlike athletic events or concerts, their services are not to be watched—they are to be experienced. Singing, sharing and praise are times for the entire congregation to become involved. While those in front carefully lead, everyone, in one way or another, is drawn into the event. Such involvement in worship should be standard fare in every local church. It is a necessary ingredient of worship that not only glorifies God, but also edifies believers.

A number of years ago, Peter Wagner, professor of church growth at Fuller Theological Seminary, wrote a book entitled, *What Are We Missing?* It was an in-depth look at the dynamic growth of Pentecostal churches in South America. As the title suggests, Wagner was looking for the "missing ingredients" in more traditional evangelical churches. One chapter in this volume is called, "It's Fun to Go to Church." He lists high-level involvement as an attraction to Pentecostal worship services. Wagner writes:

> Hardly anybody keeps track of how many persons might actually participate in a typical Pentecostal service, but one researcher took the trouble to count them at a service in Colombia, and came up with a total of 65 participants. He speculates that "if missionaries would have had their hand in this, it is unlikely the service would have followed the course it did." It is highly unlikely, because that is not the way Anglo-Saxons usually do things.

For one thing, the high quality professional training and subsequent gulf between clergy and laity that many Anglo-Saxon churches have been living with for generations have tended to cast all responsibility for leading worship on one person, the pastor. Some churches have even had to develop a "Laymen's Sunday" in a pathetic attempt to remedy the situation.

Pentecostal worshipers who do not participate in a direct way participate indirectly, but nevertheless actively. *Worship is not a passive experience. It is people-centered rather than platform-centered.* The audience participates with "Amen" and "Hallelujah" and "Praise the Lord." The Chilean Pentecostals are well-known for their threefold "Glory to God." Several times during the average service, the opportunity will come for the audience to spring to its feet, throw their arms up into the air and shout with full volume, "Gloria a Dios" three times. The total dramatic effect is breathtaking. To be honest, it's fun![26]

I am not suggesting that worship should become a free-for-all of noise, confusion and circus-like involvement. But at the same time, worship that edifies calls believers into direct and indirect participation. Men, women and children are led to individually and corporately express praise and adoration to our God. Not only does this bring Him glory, it strengthens believers. They exercise spiritual muscles, growing stronger as true followers of Jesus Christ.

The body-life movement of recent years has had a positive effect on laypeople. No longer satisfied as mere consumers, believers are calling pastors to account. Ministry is no longer accepted as the privilege and responsibility of clergy alone. Instead, laity are looking for pastors ready to equip them for service. Ministers are encouraged to see themselves more as pastor-teachers. Laypeople are the actual ministers, spiritually gifted to operate as full members of the body of Christ. Pastors are encouraged to lead and equip, letting go of more and more ministry responsibility. This emphasis is a healthy and biblical trend. At Risen King Community Church, we work to train lay people and place responsible ministry in their hands. I am convinced this is a primary factor in that congregation's tremendous growth.

Lay participation has affected all areas of church life, including worship. Pastors and leaders must recognize this trend and design worship services accordingly. The leadership base should be expanded beyond the pastoral staff, involving laypeople both indirectly and directly in the worship experience. Not only will this edify believers, it will spark a new excitement and dynamic in weekly worship. Lay involvement should include planning, preparing, praying and participating in each service.

1. *One way to expand participation is to allow people to help in the planning.* Pastors should form worship committees that evaluate, design and implement weekly services. Not only does this involve more people in worship, it lifts an unnecessary burden from the pastor. If trained properly, this committee can keep services fresh, balanced and creative. Obviously, members should be selected with great care. They should be solid disciples, sensitive to the Spirit's leading and open to change. Pastors should seek to teach these leaders a biblical philosophy of worship. Long before they are given responsibility to create dynamic services, they must have an understanding of what worship is all about. Elsewhere I have encouraged pastors to teach their people five basic concepts of corporate worship: the priority, purpose, principles, practices, and power of worship.[27]

2. *Prayer can expand people's participation in worship.*
While pastoring in Pennsylvania, I grew increasingly concerned about prayer and its relationship to dynamic worship. As a result, two important prayer ministries began in
our congregation. First, we began a prayer service preceding
each Sunday service. Early in the morning, interested
believers gathered to bathe the service in prayer. Second, a
Pastor's Prayer Corps was formed. It consisted primarily of
elderly men and women, many who attended services only
occasionally. Each week they received a letter with a list of
requests to be lifted before the Lord. The worship service
was always a top priority on this list. Not only did this
involve more people in the worship event, it regularly
unleashed an outpouring of God's Spirit upon the worship
service.

In our congregation in California, a group of Spirit-led
believers pray during our services. They meet in a separate
room, interceding for every person involved in the worship
center. Their ministry is an indispensable part of our Sunday
celebrations.

3. *Involve people in worship by involving them in the
preparation.* Laypeople can prepare for the corporate
celebration in two ways. On one hand, people are needed
for facility setup. Chairs, display tables, sound equipment
and registration packets must be ready and in order. People
can be commissioned to make banners, arrange plants
and/or fold bulletins. Doors must be opened, lights turned
on and furnaces set at appropriate levels. All these details are
opportunities for wide involvement.

4. *On yet another level, leaders must be prepared for the
service.* Special music must be selected and rehearsed. Choirs
must practice, testimonies must be prepared and lay leaders
informed of their various roles. All of this and more must

be made ready if congregations are to truly rejoice in the living King of Glory. And as they help in this preparation, laypeople grow stronger and more responsible.

5. *Finally, and most importantly, involvement in worship includes actual participation in the worship service.* This participation should be both direct and indirect. Directly, laypeople can be involved in singing in choirs, ushering, reading Scripture, praying, leading in responsive readings, delivering children's sermons and much more. In many ways, the opportunities are almost endless. Several suggestions will help keep this emphasis balanced and skillfully done.

- Do nothing on the spur of the moment, keeping all involvement well planned and prepared.
- Use gifted people, even previewing participation for adjustments or substitutions.
- Develop a basic set of guidelines that set forth expectations, attitudes and requirements for participation.
- Avoid all confusion and do only that which complements the worship theme.
- Everyone involved should be committed to giving his or her best as an offering before the Lord.

In addition, dynamic worship demands a high level of general involvement. Everyone present should be drawn into the worship experience. Week by week, leaders are to guide people through various forms of worship that demand active participation. Songs, responsive readings, prayers, praises and offerings are but a few of the ways worshipers can engage in the service.

While some people may conscientiously choose to watch, full involvement is the goal and norm. Pastors and worship leaders should place a high priority on this focus. Each service should be carefully designed so as to include specific opportunities for lay response and interaction. As stated previously, this will serve to bring vitality to services and strength to believers.

Pastors must involve the laity in the worship experience. From planning to participation, involvement can be a source of life and growth. Pastors willing to surrender leadership in such areas will be the victor for it. Soon believers will bear witness that "It's fun to go to church." Worship that edifies is worship that involves.

Integrate

I surrendered my life to the Lord while a senior in college. Like so many others, my conversion was the beginning of a brand new life. I was excited by the revelation that faith relates to all of life. Prior to knowing Christ, I felt that "religion" was something everyone should have a bit of—it helped make a person "complete." How exciting it was to learn that Christianity does not just *relate* to a part of life—it affects *all* of living. The Christian faith relates to one's relationships, hobbies, profession, goals, dreams and trials. In other words, faith becomes integrated into every single aspect of our humanity.

It is important for the local church to demonstrate that Christian faith is relevant. The worship experience should convey that truth. If worshipers are to grow strong in Christ, their experiences of praise, proclamation and response on Sunday must affect their everyday lives. The truth and experiences of Sunday must impact decisions, responses and lifestyles faced on Monday. Worship cannot be a totally transcendent focus; it must relate to life. It should address and affect real-life issues and problems. Forms of worship should be transferable from the sanctuary to the streets. The language of worship must be recognizable and understood by every listener. Not only should the worship experience relate, it must truly make a difference in people's daily lives.

Integrating worship with life has two dimensions. On the one hand, the message of the service must address real-life issues. On the other hand, the experience of worship must be transferable from Sunday to Monday, from public expression to private practice.

1. *The worship service message should address real-life issues.* God forbid that worshipers should ever respond to the Christian message with the words, "So what?" Yet often that is precisely the response. Too many preachers answer questions that no one is asking. They scratch where people seldom itch. The result is that Christianity is rejected on grounds that it is irrelevant. John Stott writes:

> A few years ago I was talking with two brothers who were students, one at Oxford University and the other at Edinburgh. They had been brought up in a traditional Christian home, both their parents being practicing Christians. But now they had renounced their parents' faith and their Christian upbringing. One was a complete atheist, he told me; the other preferred to call himself an agnostic. What had happened? I asked. Was it that they no longer believed Christianity to be true? "No," they replied, "that's not our problem. We're not really interested to know whether Christianity is true. And if you were able to convince us that it is, we're not at all sure we would embrace it." "What is your problem, then?" I asked with some astonishment. "What we want to know," they went on, "is not whether Christianity is true, but whether it's relevant. And frankly we don't see

how it can be. Christianity was born two millennia ago in a first-century Palestinian culture. What can an ancient religion of the Middle East say to us who live in the exciting kaleidoscopic world of the end of the twentieth century? We have men on the moon in the seventies, and shall have men on Mars in the eighties, transplant surgery today and genetic engineering tomorrow. What possible relevance can a primitive Palestinian religion have for us?"[28]

The Christian faith is precisely what people need today. We all know that. But many preachers fail to bring the truths of Scripture into the world of today. That is a critical error. Sensitive pastors seek to expose themes and messages of Scripture that speak to people where they live. They are careful to deal with real-life issues. While thoroughly scriptural, they are completely relevant. This takes both good exegesis of Scripture and a sensitive interpretation of life. With the skill of a weaver, the pastor integrates the Word of God into the life of the worshiper. Once that happens, the believer carries the message with him in life. It helps him respond to life's problems, overcome life's trials and make life's decisions from a Christian perspective. Themes of worship must be developed with this concept of integration always in mind.

Pastors may find it helpful to survey their people or establish a lay committee that would assist in identifying the critical issues being faced by their members. Certainly this is not meant as a substitute to the Spirit's leading, but rather a channel of His guidance. (I highly recommend *The Baby Boomerang*, by Doug Murren, on this topic. The author addresses the matter of contemporary relevance in the church, with particular reference to the baby-boomer generation. This resource is available through Regal Books.)

2. *Integration involves carrying worship from the sanctuary to the street.* Christian worship is not an exclusively corporate Sunday morning activity. It is to be our lifestyle seven days a week. More important, it must be seen as the top priority of healthy Christian living.

In his book, *Lord, Make My Life a Miracle*, Ray Ortlund speaks of three priorities of the Christian life: commitment to Christ, commitment to the body of Christ, commitment to the work of Christ in the world. Note that the first commitment of our lives is to Christ. And the first ingredient of maintaining that commitment is daily worship.

Edifying believers involves teaching them to be, first and foremost, worshipers. This lesson not only affects their personal walk with the Lord, it raises up a people more deeply committed to corporate worship. They learn the power of putting Christ first in their lives. But such integration does not just happen, it must be developed strategically by pastors and church leaders.

First, worship should be the initial response whenever and wherever the church gathers. Meetings should begin with worship before any business takes place. It should consume the first moments of choir practice, Bible studies, youth meetings, cell groups and fellowship dinners. Wherever two or more gather, worship must be the first response. This sends a clear message of integration to the congregation.

Second, people should be taught that worship is top priority in the believer's life. A book like Ortlund's can be a great study resource or discussion guide to that end.

Third, people must be equipped to actually make worship part of daily living. Help them with their private praise and adoration. Laypeople need teaching on how to structure a quality devotional time that prioritizes worship. Numerous resources are available today that can help in that process. I have found Dick Eastman's *A Celebration of Praise* particularly helpful.

Integration in worship does not just happen. It takes hard work and sensitive leadership. Pastors and laypeople must have their finger on the pulse of life issues. They must deal with life's problems. Principles of Christian living must be transferred to daily practice. The reality of the Christian faith must be communicated in clear, relevant terms. It is the only way that the experience of worship will actually make a positive difference in the lives of people.

Discussion Questions

1. List all the synonyms of edify that come to your mind.
2. What is Arrested Spiritual Development? Is your church in any way suffering from this disease? What are the evidences?
3. List the specific areas of Christian faith and practice that need to be addressed in your congregation.
4. How would you rate your worship services?
   Dry 1 2 3 4 5 6 7 8 9 Inspiring
5. What changes would you suggest to make your services more exciting?
6. Consider developing a survey for your congregation to evaluate the weekly sermon. How would the people/pastor respond to such an activity? What questions would you ask?
7. What suggestions would you make to help listeners better understand and remember the sermon each week?
8. How many people are directly involved in the weekly worship experience, planning, praying, preparing, participating?

9. Write a set of guidelines for worship service participants. Consider attitudes, understandings and approaches to leadership.
10. Make a list of "real-life" issues you feel should be addressed in worship over the next three months.

CHAPTER

6

Will This Worship Service Appeal to Visitors?

FIRST IMPRESSIONS COUNT! And for most people, their first impressions of a local church are shaped by the worship service. More often than not, a Sunday morning service is the first place visitors are exposed to a congregation. They may be brought by a friend or attend as recent arrivals in the community. Regardless of how they come, worship is usually the first stop. What they see, hear and feel in this service sends a message about the life and vitality of the congregation. That experience helps people decide if they will return or stay away. Simply put, the worship service has a direct effect on local church growth.

One summer I was invited to teach a short-term course at a Canadian seminary. Since I would be there over two weekends, I decided to visit several churches in the area. This is a great way to get new and fresh ideas on worship and church growth. But my plans changed after visiting the first church. The event was so wonderful and refreshing that I went back to the same church for my entire stay. From the time I pulled into the parking lot until I left for the hotel, I felt welcomed, comfortable and spiritually refreshed. The first experience was so good, I wanted to repeat it.

Pastors and church leaders need to recognize that worship is a key ingredient in church growth. Services must be designed that appeal to visitors, drawing them to Christ and to His church. My Canadian experience is similar to that of most visitors. A family moves into a community and begins to search for a church home. They visit several congregations, evaluating and deciding. The level of warmth, excitement and vitality invariably determines the next step. If positive, they choose to return. If the experience makes them uncomfortable, they will in most cases go elsewhere.

The worship service is not just important in attracting new people to your church. It also has a significant effect on people's openness to the gospel. Obviously, not all visitors are newcomers to your community. Not all are shopping for a church. Many are unbelievers brought by friends or seeking help during a personal crisis. A dynamic worship service can help draw them to Christ. It can convince them that there is something genuine and exciting behind the message. Seeing believers enthusiastic and attentive in worship convinces unbelievers that the gospel is valid. Thus, the worship service becomes a critical part of local church evangelism. British Anglican Michael Green writes:

> In the passage in First Corinthians, which we have noted earlier, the expected result of Spirit-filled worship is the conversion of people who come in. In the case of the Antiochene church of Acts 13, it is the same pattern; mission follows hard on the heels of Spirit-led worship. The point is important, because *there are few such powerful evangelistic agencies as a Christian fellowship at worship, where the various gifts of the Spirit are being*

*exercised in love and harmony by people who are consciously
under the leadership of that same Spirit.*[29]

This then is our fourth and final imperative for worship
that would be dynamic: the weekly service must appeal to
visitors. Pastors and church leaders must take this issue to
heart. Serious steps should be taken to draw people to Christ
and to His church through worship. Obviously, the three
emphases discussed in earlier chapters directly affect this
appeal. Life and vitality are evident in worship that glorifies
God, focuses on Christ and edifies believers. But leaders
interested in outreach and evangelism go a step further. For
these visitors who do not yet know Christ personally, they
design worship services that are comfortable, clear, convincing and creative. We will look at these four important
ingredients.

Comfortable

The following story is not pleasant. In some ways, I would
rather not share it. Yet it illustrates the tragic consequences
of worship services that do not appeal to visitors. It is in no
way an isolated incident. Similar events take place each
Sunday in churches across the country. And for many
people, eternal issues are at stake.

A Christian young man in a certain church was burdened
for his family. A new convert, he regularly witnessed to his
parents. Although they were tolerant of his new-found faith,
his parents were not interested in the Lord. Their world was
quite all right as it was.

For months, the young man prayed that some door would
open to give his family broader exposure to Christians. He
was particularly interested in getting them to a church event.
There they could meet others "like him" and possibly

become interested in Christ Jesus. When his mother, who liked music and frequently attended concerts, agreed to attend a special Sunday evening concert featuring a Christian musician, the young man was overjoyed.

As it turned out, the mother arrived alone to find the church already well filled. She slipped into a pew with several other people, none of whom she knew. But for a concert, that presented no problem.

Unfortunately, there was confusion as to the goal of the evening. The pastoral staff, knowing there would be unbelievers in the audience, expected music and a gospel presentation. But the musician must have assumed everyone present was already a Christian. Early in the service, he asked people to gather in groups of three and four. They were to share their burdens and then pray about the stated concerns. For most Christians, such an exercise would be acceptable. But visitors would find this sort of thing far too intimidating. And that was precisely the reaction of the young man's mother. As soon as the directive was given, she rose from her pew and left the sanctuary. It was too much too soon. She had been made to feel uncomfortable. Not likely will she adventure again into that church.

The Christians in attendance evaluated the evening positively, particularly those who regularly attended that church. In many ways the worship service was powerful. Certainly God was glorified, Christ magnified and believers left inspired. But someone failed to consider one other critical element of dynamic worship—the service was not designed to appeal to visitors. As a result, unbelievers were made to feel uncomfortable. It was a tragic mistake—one that could have eternal consequences. It was a mistake we cannot afford to make.

Pastors and leaders must work at making visitors feel

welcome and at ease. My experience is that visitors already feel a bit uptight before they arrive. Going to a new church for the first time is not easy. For many people, all they need is one obstacle—one uncomfortable situation—to make them decide not to return.

The task of the leader is to make the worship service a positive, non-threatening experience for visitors. All potential obstacles—every situation that could cause insecurity— must be addressed and eliminated. What follows is a discussion of several such items. For the most part, the matters listed are practical rather than spiritual concerns. In fact, they deal primarily with matters that lead up to and follow the actual worship experience. Yet the way in which they are addressed determines how comfortable visitors will feel.

1. *The first obstacle that faces visitors is the visibility of the local church.* When people decide to visit a church, they must be able to easily find the building. The newspaper ad may be inviting, but if visitors have difficulty locating the church, they will more often than not turn and go home. Remember, it only takes one obstacle—one reason for people to change their minds. They may search for a while, but it does not take long for them to say, "I give up; I'm just not going." When I am asked to consult on church growth, this is the first thing I look at. How easy is it to find this church?

Churches located on side streets, away from the main flow of traffic, have problems. They are usually hard for people to find. As I see it, such churches have two options in solving this problem. The best way to handle it is to relocate. Find property on a main traffic artery. Too many church locations are determined by economic considerations. The first question asked is, "Where can we find a piece of affordable property?" Leaders must learn that that is a costly decision. Though the land or building may be cheap, the results are costly. Visitors will not be a regular part of morning worship.

I recently spoke in a new church, planted in a mid-size New York town. Once I arrived in the community, it took me 20 minutes to find the church. Even with directions it was a frustration. Because of limited finances, local leaders had purchased an old building five streets away from the main thoroughfare. A maze of one-way streets and alleys discourage even the serious visitors. Although I hope to see the church grow, I have serious doubts about its long-term future in that location.

Not all churches can face relocation. In that case, the next best option is to mark the route with signs. Clearly identify the direction from main streets to the church building, making sure to identify every turn. Use large signs, consistent in format. Be sure to have a sign in front of the church that leaves no questions about it being "the place." Also, in all publicity, include clear directions. Highlight familiar landmarks so visitors can readily identify the general location.

2. *Churches wanting visitors to regularly attend worship service must provide adequate parking.* The basic rule of thumb is that 20 percent of your parking spaces should be empty at peak hours. Visitors tend to come late. If there is not easy and adequate parking when they arrive, you are likely to lose them. I found it difficult persuading my church leaders that this was important. Finally, they noticed people slowly driving through our lot, searching for a space. Finding none available, they would drive out the back gate and never return. Soon, the first of three parking-lot projects was underway.

Churches facing parking problems have several options.

Obviously, they may not be able to add parking space. Another solution is to identify a reasonable number of spaces, close to the main door, for visitors only. Ask faithful members to park at a distance, so that room in the main lot can be freed up. This may be difficult at first, but the pastor's example can help motivate church leaders.

The church can also provide parking-lot helpers who give instructions for double and triple parking. While not the best solution, with clear directions, people will feel safe in blocking others. Remember, if spaces are unavailable, your church is losing people before they ever walk through the door.

3. *Getting to the door and sanctuary is the next issue.* Most churches have multiple entrances. For regular members, that is no problem, but visitors may be unsure of the door that leads to the sanctuary. All of us are uncomfortable with the unknown. "Does that door lead to the sanctuary, or will I walk into a meeting and embarrass myself?" Such feelings are real and must be disarmed before they ever arise. Directions from parking lot to sanctuary must be clearly identified. While signs are good, people in parking lots are better. With minimum training, laypeople can briefly welcome visitors as they walk toward the building. They can answer questions and provide ready information about services, nurseries and sanctuary location.

4. *Churches concerned about visitor "comfort" provide greeters at designated entrances.* Their role is to greet visitors and assure them that they are welcome. Basic instructions can make this a positive and important ministry. Greeters should be encouraged to smile and welcome newcomers, introduce themselves and then ask the visitors their names. When time permits, a short discussion about their backgrounds can put people at ease. Obviously, greeters should

give directions to the sanctuary, nursery or children's church. It helps to have them identified with a name tag of some sort. A greeting network is easy to develop. Couples and singles can serve a month at a time. This provides broad involvement in the congregation. Depending on the setting and culture, standards of dress and decorum should be maintained.

5. *Churches concerned about visitors provide first-class nursery care.* I cannot over-emphasize this point. This one issue alone can determine a family's future interest in a particular local church. Infants and toddlers are priceless to parents. Visitors are extremely reluctant to leave their children under the care of someone they do not know. If there is any question about the quality of care, any reason to suspect confusion or risk, anxiety levels soar. I know, for we have three children of our own and have experienced those fears. In fact, if there were two churches similar in quality, but one had a first-class nursery and the other did not, we would choose the one with the quality nursery care every time. And believe me, most visitors with small children feel exactly the same way.

Quality infant-toddler care begins with easy directions to the nursery. Signs and greeters should clearly point the way. Be sure the room is pleasant and well-equipped. It should be carpeted, bright and as "childproof" as possible. Equipment and toys should be first-class, clean and in good repair. There should be an abundant supply of diapers (cloth and disposable), crib sheets and first-aid supplies. Nursery workers should be pleasant and mature. Several churches have nurses, in uniform, serving as baby-sitters. Their presence can immediately put parents at ease. Teenagers can help but should never be primarily responsible. All workers must seem excited about serving visitors and their children.

Visitors should be given a brief tour of the room. It helps if workers are trained to inquire of parents regarding preferences and special concerns. I was particularly impressed with one nursery worker. She asked to accompany us to the sanctuary. She wanted to know where we would be seated and assured us that if the need arose, she would come and get us.

Finally, be sure that when parents return to the nursery, they find their child "clothed and in his or her right mind." A clean diaper and pleasant baby go a long way to draw visitors back. All of this enables visitors to comfortably experience the worship service. Trust me. This is one investment in growth that churches must make!

6. *Provide ushers that really usher.* It is not enough to have men silently standing at the sanctuary entrance handing out bulletins. Nor will it do for them to just point out empty seats in sections of the auditorium, particularly when it means visitors must climb over people to sit down. Good ushers usher! They lead people to an available pew, and introduce the visitors to the people sitting nearby.

If the service is to start soon, people should be seated toward the rear of the church. It is embarrassing for visitors to have to walk the length of the aisle. I have visited churches where ushers rope off the last one or two pews. Since most visitors arrive close to or after the beginning of the service, this gives unnoticeable access to seats. Some of the "faithful" might need to release territory to make this possible!

7. *Churches need to identify visitors in a non-threatening way.* I was once asked to advise a church on its worship service. The congregation was healthy and the service vibrant. The church often had visitors, but most came once and never returned. It did not take long to discover why. It was the way they welcomed visitors. First, they attached a

six-inch, bright yellow visitor banner to all newcomers. That alone was unbecoming and embarrassing—it simply drew too much attention to the person. But the worst was yet to come.

Early in the service, visitors were asked to stand. They were to give their names and tell where they lived. This by itself is threatening to most people, but then came the "last straw." In order to express love and gratitude to the visitors, a few members would join hands around them, look into their eyes and sing, "We love you with the love of the Lord." These church people were sincere. But it was just too much. Spotlighting visitors like this turned them off and away.

Visitors must be identified for follow-up purposes. But it should be a pleasant experience. A Nazarene church known to me uses this procedure. Visitors enter the front door and are greeted immediately. Next, they are led to a table where a hostess records their names and addresses. After welcoming them, she places a small, attractive adhesive-backed rose on them. She explains that this identifies them as visitors. Before moving to the sanctuary, they receive a packet of information and a small gift.

People in the congregation have been trained to look for these "roses." Following the service, members go out of their way to welcome them. Several people are prepared to invite visitors home to share a meal. No pressure, of course, just a friendly opportunity. Visitors are asked if they would like a tour of the facility and a description of various ministries. The process is positive and leaves a good impression. Churches can introduce this idea with minimum effort. It is a small investment that pays extremely high dividends.

These seven issues are crucial to the weekly worship experience. Though primarily practical, they address significant issues concerning visitor appeal. In many ways, they help close the "evangelistic back door" in the local church. Begin to initiate them at once. Worship that appeals to visitors is comfortable. Pastors and church leaders must accept that standard and invest time and resources to make it so.

Clear

Jason was my best friend all through grade school. Like many boys that age, we were virtually inseparable. Whenever possible, we spent time together, playing baseball, building forts or watching our favorite television programs. Occasionally I would even attend church with him and his family. To this day I can remember some distinct impressions those church visits left on me. Jason attended an Episcopalian church, rich in liturgy and symbol. Two memories stand out as I reflect back on those experiences. First, I was amazed that everyone but me seemed to know when to sit, stand, sing or pray. There were no obvious cues from the priests, yet the people knew what to do! Second, I found the liturgy interesting but had no idea what the actions meant. As a result, aside from arousing my curiosity a bit, the services had little effect on me.

My lack of understanding was not merely a result of boyhood. That church, as with all congregations, had a language totally foreign to the "outsider." Though second nature to its members, their actions were uncommon to me and their symbols without meaning. Believe it or not, most visitors have the same feeling and frustration when visiting *your* church! No matter how informal the service may be, the worship experience can leave the unbeliever bewildered and frustrated. Evangelicals use words that have ambiguous meanings in the secular world. Our songs are unfamiliar. Our forms of worship are burdening. We refer to Scripture passages as if everyone can easily locate them in the Bible. And our actions, though filled with meaning to the believer, make little sense to the uninformed observer.

Worship services that appeal to visitors must be clear. Pastors and leaders should work hard at defining, explaining and simplifying their services. Though it takes sensitivity and patience, all forms of worship should be shaped with the unchurched in mind. If visitors are a regular part of worship, care must be taken to insure meaning and under-standing. I would like to make several suggestions that can help leaders at this point. Please do not assume that only highly liturgical churches need to take these precautions. Every congregation interested in growth must take note.

1. *The starting point of clarity is with the language of worship.* Christians do, in fact, have a language all their own. Some people refer to it as "Christianese." We constantly throw around terms like salvation, new birth, justification, sanctification, regeneration, atonement, righteousness and original sin. On and on the words go, words full of meaning yet the meaning is totally missed by unbelievers if the words are spoken without definition. Even evangelistic messages are filled with such words. It may be Good News, but if spoken in a foreign tongue it does not mean a thing.

Preachers must take time to review their sermons. Wherever these words are found, pastors should substitute or define. The language of preaching must be familiar to every listener. John Wesley had a great concern for clarity. He would often read his sermons to an uneducated servant girl. She was to stop him whenever a word or phrase was unfamiliar. Why? Because Wesley wanted his sermons to have meaning to the poor, the illiterate and the down-trod-den. Pastors would do well to learn from this model. Friends and family can help preachers fit their messages to the context of the unchurched listener. It is a critical investment toward proclaiming a "clear" word from the Lord.

2. *Time must be taken in the service to define and explain the various forms of worship.* Not everyone knows why there are doxologies, offerings, altar prayers or communion celebrations. Certainly Christians understand the importance of baptism, but does the unchurched visitor? I think not. With minimum effort, however, the leader can give them an adequate explanation. Pastors and leaders must accept the responsibility for clarifying the symbolic acts of worship. Remember, if we fail to explain, visitors may draw their own conclusions. Often, these uninformed conclusions lead to gross misunderstandings.

John E. Stevey, dean of students at Alliance Theological Seminary, tells an interesting story illustrating the danger of misunderstanding. He decided to make a large metal Christian and Missionary Alliance logo—an arrangement of a cross, pitcher, laver and crown, representing the fourfold gospel of Christ—for the outside of the new addition to the seminary. An unchurched friend was visiting John and saw the piece in his workshop.

"John," he remarked, "I understand the wine glass and the pitcher of beer, but what do the T and W stand for?" John was glad to correct his friend's misunderstanding, but had he seen that symbol in worship, what conclusions might he have drawn?

I would like to make two suggestions that can help bring clarity to worship services. First, occasionally take time to explain the more "unintelligible" forms of worship. Such an explanation need not take a long time or be done every week. But regularly inform visitors of the rich meaning behind the symbols and expressions of worship. You will find that even church members appreciate these interpretations. Also, consider printing a visitor's guide to worship. I have included a copy of one example in Appendix A. Key questions, often asked by visitors, are answered. This eliminates misunderstandings and enables unbelievers to better appreciate the worship service.

3. *Churches have a ready-made resource for clarity in the weekly worship bulletin.* The bulletin can lead the visitor step-by-step through the worship service. Choose a cover that is visually attractive. Using a top-quality paper and a simple format, develop a clear, easy-to-follow outline of the service. Avoid unnecessary "Christianese." Do not pack bulletins with calendars, updates and committee meeting announcements. Be careful what you write in the bulletin, remembering that visitors will be reading it. Always include a pleasant word of welcome to all visitors. If at all possible, have the bulletin professionally printed. Members already know the general format for the service. Shape your weekly bulletin for visitors.

4. *Singing is another place in which we must work for clarity on behalf of visitors.* Christians, for the most part, enjoy singing. It is a form of worship rooted in the first-century church. But if we are not careful, congregational singing can make visitors uncomfortable. In the first place, our hymns are often from another generation. They do not always communicate readily to the unchurched. Granted, we cannot and would not want to throw out classic hymns just because unbelievers are not familiar with them. We should, though, sing songs that can reach the contemporary listener. Second, spontaneous chorus singing can leave the visitor behind. Without words or music, the visitor becomes an uncomfortable observer. Overheads and chorus books, professionally produced within the limits of copyright laws, are a must. They add clarity to the experience, encouraging

the visitor to join in the celebration.

5. *I would encourage pastors and church leaders to use clear, modern translations of Scripture in their worship services.* In 1987, The Christian and Missionary Alliance planted 101 churches in the United States on Easter Sunday. Their target group was the unchurched. Worship services were predominately non-traditional, appealing to the contemporary, secular audience. Every church was given Bibles for distribution. They were the *New International Version.* The King James Version has a rich tradition, but it is not easy for the uninitiated to comprehend. With the New International Version, language is not a barrier. It is equally helpful to list the page number of any texts in the bulletin. We all remember the frustrations of flipping forever and never finding Habbakuk or Philippians. A common pew Bible keeps the whole flock on course. If the pastor cross-references, he simply calls out text and page. Everyone, including the most uninformed visitor is able to keep pace. What a tremendous appeal! What a simple yet decisive step for clarity.

The sensitive worship committee is committed to clarity. These suggestions are but the starting point for appealing worship services. But these first steps must be taken if visitors are to understand and embrace the experiences of Christian worship. Certainly this takes work. But as with so much already discussed, the benefits are far-reaching. They may be, in fact, eternal.

Convincing

"Actions speak louder than words." How many times that phrase has been shared as a warning to Christians. Right belief is important, but people watch how we live more than they listen to what we say. If our actions contradict the truths we confess, people reject our words and believe what they see.

This is just as true for worship services. Proclaiming life and truth is of little benefit when the worship experience is dull and boring. On the other hand, dynamic worship can convince visitors that our faith is not only right, it is real. Dynamic worship sends a clear message that God is alive and at work, changing people by His power. Then and only then will visitors be attracted to the local church and its message of new life in Christ Jesus.

Martyn Lloyd-Jones emphasizes that point in his book, *Joy Unspeakable*. He writes,

> What I am trying to put to you is this: I am certain that the world outside is not going to pay much attention to all the organized efforts of the Christian church. The one thing she will pay attention to is a body of people filled with this spirit of rejoicing. That is how Christianity conquered the ancient world. It was this amazing joy of these people. Even when you threw them into prison, or even to death, it did not matter, they went on rejoicing; rejoicing in tribulations.[30]

If worship services are to appeal to visitors, they must grab people's attention. The spirit of rejoicing, of life, of victory must be evident among worshipers. Unbelievers should have no option but to conclude that our message is true and deserves acceptance.

Pastors and church leaders must design worship services that are just that—convincing. Visitors should see that worshipers are enthusiastic and committed to their Lord. They must sense a difference, a dynamic presence of God's power in the service. And they should hear the Christian gospel loud and clear—God changes people's lives. Obviously, the Holy Spirit does the work of convincing in the unbelieving heart. But worship leaders must include forms of worship that can be channels for the Spirit's power. I suggest several such channels as key ingredients to worship that convinces.

1. *Services should be positive and upbeat.* They should convey an atmosphere of joy and excitement. As stated in chapter four, worshipers must be enthusiastic, celebrating our risen Savior. Heartfelt praise and adoration sends a powerful message to unbelieving observers. Rather than sensing a dead ritual, they experience the Living Lord of resurrection power. Special music, songs and sermons should emphasize victorious themes. Pastors must work hard at designing services that generate life. Visitors are then impacted by the reality of the gospel, attracted to Christ and His church.

Conveying a positive message may be more important in this generation than ever before. The excesses of the seventies and eighties have resulted in wholesale brokenness in the nineties. Pastor Doug Murren writes,

> In times past the human spirit was far more sturdy than it is now. Modernity has taken a high toll on the human spirit. . . . The stress of modern life has had a greatly negative impact on the self esteem of modern man.[31]

Quite frankly, people do not come to church to hear about bad news and brokenness. They enter churches hoping for some good news, and certainly we have the message they are dying to hear!

2. *Remember that personal testimonies can be powerful.* Visitors should hear from "unpaid religious people." Few things convince unbelievers of the power of Christ as does the personal witness. Visitors can hear firsthand how God

changes lives. Worshipers can witness to forgiveness, provision, healing and hope. Many of the unbelievers present are yearning for these very realities. Laypeople, sharing about God's touch, declare that He is the answer to life's perplexities and problems. Such testimonies of God's grace can attract people to the Lord.

One of my favorite churches is in an urban setting. It is a fast-growing black congregation that majors in excitement. Each week they have an extended time for personal testimonies. The pastor asks the question, "What has God been doing in your life?" People stand, enthusiastically giving praise for God's provision. After each testimony, they sing a chorus entitled, "God's Not Dead, He's Still Living." The lyrics are simple, but the message is clear.

> God's not dead, He's still living
> God's not dead, He's still living
> God's not dead, He's still living
> I can feel Him in my hands
> I can feel Him in my feet
> I can feel Him all over me.

Over and over they sing that chorus. By testimony and song, the congregation repeatedly declares the glory and grace of God. Be assured of this: visitors leave that church each week with one dominant message ringing in their ears—"God is not dead, He's still living." In truth, though the vehicle varies, that should be the goal of every service.

3. *Answered prayer can convince visitors of God's power.* Week by week churches across the world pray in worship for people's needs. Requests are given for guidance, comfort, healing, provision and protection. Most services include a time for public prayer when these concerns are lifted before

the Lord. This practice is good. It is a display of faith and trust in a God who cares. But we must go a step further in worship. Time should be taken to highlight answers to prayer. Not only will this encourage believers, it can convince visitors of God's power. It will cause them to turn to the God who is able.

4. *Preaching is a key channel for the Spirit's work of convincing.* Relevant messages that speak to genuine life issues attract people to Christ's church. Visitors might expect boring, out-of-touch sermons. True biblical preaching, rooted in the contemporary world, however, will surprise them. Visitors see that the teachings of Scripture make sense for today. They see that Scripture speaks to depression, hopelessness, confusion, family relationships and many other issues. People are soon convinced that God's Word addresses life's questions head-on. It provides the answers they so desperately need.

5. *Ministering to people during the worship service is another way to convince unbelievers.* By that I mean actually praying for people to be healed physically and emotionally. There is much discussion these days on the relationship of signs and wonders to church growth. Across the globe people are being attracted to the church by demonstrations of God's power. In some places, whole people-groups are turning to Christ because of a healing, a deliverance or some other miraculous sign.

For several years Fuller Theological Seminary offered a course on signs and wonders. The class dealt with biblical, theological and historical perspectives on this subject. John Wimber, leader in the Vineyard Movement, played an important role in the Fuller experience. The basic thesis of the signs and wonders theme is that people are attracted to the gospel when they see that the kingdom of God is more powerful than the kingdom of darkness.

Few people would disagree with this basic theme. Much debate goes on, however, as to the validity of signs and wonders for today. I would encourage pastors and leaders to examine this matter openly and prayerfully. God *is* more powerful than Satan and *is* willing to set people free. And how desperately people outside of Christ need to be set free. This freedom can extend from the spiritual to the emotional and physical. But we must step out in faith as vessels of His power.

Belief in healing is fundamental to Christian and Missionary Alliance theology. This belief must be put into practice by regularly praying for God's touch upon people's lives. Times of healing in worship, when approached sensitively, can be deeply moving. Not only can people be touched by prayer, unbelievers can be attracted to the God of resurrection power.

I pastor a congregation that is convinced God still moves in power today. Each week during the worship service individuals are invited to receive prayer for special needs. People are instructed to stand, while the remainder of the congregation waits silently before God. Trained ministry teams are commissioned to go to those standing, interview them regarding their needs, and pray. In this congregation's short history, countless people have been touched by the Lord. Quite regularly, following this ministry of prayer, an invitation is given for individuals to receive Christ. Knowing that God's presence is powerfully evident and experienced, the opportunity is made for evangelism. In one 12 month period, over 90 adults transferred their loyalty from the Kingdom of Darkness to the Kingdom of Light! Why? Because their experience of worship convinced them of God's power.

Church leaders should carefully implement this emphasis in worship. It must be backed by prayer and study. The focal point is not the healing, but the Divine Healer. With adequate thought and preparation, this step of faith can lead congregations to new dimensions in growth and excitement. Realistically, why should unbelievers turn to Christ if He does not have the power to set them free from Satan's domain? But, of course, we know He does. And we should demonstrate that truth by praying regularly and publicly for those who are broken, in bondage and battered. Soon, convinced of God's power, unbelievers will turn in faith and believe.

Creative

There are two challenges pastors and worship leaders face each week. They must get visitors' attention, and they must hold their interest throughout the service. *That* is a big order. To do this, leaders must consistently design worship services that are creative. It demands variety in form, color, sound and movement. This will not only increase attention levels, visitors will be attracted enough by the service to return for another experience.

Most Christian people reject the idea that worship must be entertaining. While not a show, worship services must keep moving if they are to hold people's attention. Remember your neighbor, "Old Uncle Bill," who sits in front of the television hour after hour. He watches highly creative entertainment, filled with color, sound and plenty of action. His attention level is short, so programs move quickly from one scene to the next. His memory is poor, so advertisers sell their products with emotional appeal and repetition. If he ever comes to church, "Old Uncle Bill" will not be so easily moved or challenged. Neither friends nor traditions will hold him. It will take prayer and plenty of creativity.

1. *Creativity in worship begins with variety.* As I have said before, each service should have a dominant theme—the single message you want to drive into the listener's heart. While you may be saying one thing, creativity demands that you say it in many different ways. You cannot just preach a theme, have testimonies on it and provide special music that declares it. Visitors should see banners that highlight the theme, hear illustrations that clarify the theme and prayers that embody the theme. The message is stated and restated. This variety not only reinforces a biblical truth, it keeps the visitor attentive. Movement from one form of worship to the next draws the person deeper and deeper into the experience.

2. *Worship leaders would do well to remember that visual stimuli capture a person's attention.* Creative use of color can keep worship services appealing. A pleasant atmosphere should be created with festive banners. It can enhance a sense of celebration, inducing a spirit of excitement and expectation.

Paul Bostaph is director of drama and design at Risen King Community Church. With a secular background in both theater and graphic arts, Paul serves to create beauty and movement in our worship services. Though the congregation meets in an industrial warehouse, the atmosphere is attractive and inspiring. At Mr. Bostaph's supervision, colorful banners were hung throughout the 10,000-square-foot worship center. Each, beautifully designed and made, focuses upon an Old Testament name of God. The banners add to the "feeling" of celebration and life. In addition, thematic murals are painted on the walls, adding to the visual impact upon the worshiper. Visitors regularly make positive comments about this ministry, convincing me of its importance and effectiveness.

3. *Sound is an ally of creative worship.* It often ministers when all else fails. More than once I have seen hardened hearts melted by anointed music. Pastors must be committed to quality music in the service. Early in my ministry, people would volunteer to sing in church. Not wanting to offend, I would invariably allow them. Unfortunately, not everyone who wanted to sing was gifted to do so. Relatives may have found their ministry appealing, but most visitors were not impressed. Their focus easily drifted from the service.

Though it is difficult to do, previewing all music and restricting participation is necessary. I still gave people opportunity to sing, but not in the worship service. There, everything was to be done by people gifted in that form of ministry. Was there opposition? Of course! But with patience and diplomacy most members of the congregation were convinced the policy was good. Remember, if services fail to touch their lives, visitors may be there for the first and last time. With that much at stake, an investment in creativity and quality is critically important.

4. *Drama can be used to creatively communicate God's truth.* I first experienced drama in worship while studying with David Watson at Fuller Theological Seminary. His team used short skits to illustrate key points in Watson's sermons. These came either before the message began, or as dramatic interludes within his presentation. The impact upon the audience was amazing to watch. People saw living illustrations of biblical principles, making God's truth relevant to life situations. I quickly went from skeptic to believer, regularly using drama within the worship service.

Though the kingdom of darkness uses drama to evil effect, drama can be an effective means of presenting the gospel to unbelievers. In an almost unexpected way, key truths bypass defenses and go straight to the heart. Numerous helpful resources are available at local Christian bookstores. Watson's group published two books, *Time to Act* and *Lightening Sketches*, filled with skits and short dramas suitable for worship. Both are available through Hodder and Stoughton Publishers in England. I encourage pastors to prayerfully consider adding drama as a form of communication in worship. In a visually dominated culture such as ours, it will only serve to enhance the creative appeal of the worship service.

The possibilities for creativity in worship are almost limitless. But it demands prayer, planning and innovation. Pastors must be committed to designing worship services that appeal to visitors. It is more than a mere opportunity to capture the attention. It is an obligation with eternal consequences.

Discussion Questions

1. How would you evaluate the following on a scale of 1 to 10 (10 being the best)?
   Your church's visibility _____
   Parking _____
   Directions to the sanctuary _____
   Quality of nursery care _____
   Training of ushers _____
   What would you do to improve these things?
2. How are visitors identified in your church? Do you feel the process is at all embarrassing?
3. Make a tape of one of your worship services. Listen to the service with your wife or some other honest critic, making a list of all "Christianese" that goes undefined.

4. Is your bulletin a clear guide for visitors? How could it be improved?
5. List all forms of worship that may be ambiguous or confusing to visitors. How could you explain them?
6. How would members of your congregation respond to modern-translation pew Bibles? In what ways would such Bibles benefit newcomers?
7. What does your worship service convey through the singing, praying, preaching and ministering? Would visitors perceive life in it or dead orthodoxy?
8. What changes should be made in the service to make it more "convincing"?
9. How could times of healing be included in the morning worship?
10. What creative changes should you make to hold visitors' interest?

Where Does This All Begin?

I RECEIVED SOME GOOD ADVICE from a district super-intendent. He had invited me to speak on worship at a district pastor's conference. My lectures were built upon the principles outlined in this book. The presentations went well, and almost everyone felt the study was helpful. The superintendent attended all the sessions and was com-plimentary at the end. He commented that the material was balanced and practical. His input pleased me, and I thanked the Lord for the opportunity to serve Him in this way.

Several weeks later, the same superintendent telephoned me to ask for an appointment. We met a few days later, and he shared with me some valid concerns he had about the conference. His comments did not focus on the material itself. Rather, a few pastors had taken what was said and tried to change every aspect of their church's worship im-mediately. They redid too much too soon. As a result, some laypeople were intimidated. This led to serious conflicts within those churches. The superintendent felt I needed to advise pastors *how* to implement change in worship.

Be assured that I accepted his counsel. I studied my presentation and decided to add a basic outline for im-plementation. I am including those 10 steps here and hope that readers will find them a helpful starting point. They are intended as a guide, translating worship principles into balanced, realistic practice.

1. *Pastors must take time to seriously study the biblical, historical and practical dimensions of Christian worship.* Obviously there is much more to an adequate understanding of worship than this book provides. Any of the volumes listed on the bibliography can be used. As a starting point I suggest:

> *Worship Is a Verb*, by Robert Webber
> *Worship Old and New*, by Robert Webber
> *Worship in the Early Church*, by Ralph Martin
> *Worship: Rediscovering the Missing Jewel*, by Allen and Borror
> *O Come Let Us Worship*, by Robert Rayburn
> *The Encyclopedia of Worship*, edited by Robert Webber
> *Whatever Happened to Worship*, by A.W. Tozer

From this study, pastors should develop a philosophy of worship that will serve as the foundation for everything that a congregation does in worship. This book can serve as a useful guide in that process.

2. *Pastors should prayerfully select people to serve on a church worship committee.* This committee would be responsible to evaluate and design the weekly services. It is critical that members be spiritually mature, committed to dynamic worship and open to change. The pastor and the committee should meet each week. Adequate time should be provided for prayer and thoughtful preparation. It is best to plan services at least one month in advance.

3. *This committee should be taught about the biblical, historical and practical dynamics of Christian worship.* The pastor should set aside a time, preferably a retreat, for this

training. He can share the insights gained from his own study. In addition, the pastor should communicate his personal philosophy of worship. Out of that retreat, the committee should formulate the church's philosophy and guidelines for worship. Such a document is invaluable. It serves as the basic blueprint for all decisions regarding the worship service.

4. *Evaluate the present worship service, including a congregational survey.* The pastor and worship committee should develop a basic questionnaire for the congregation. Every aspect of the existing worship service should be covered. In addition, evaluate the service in light of the principles outlined in this book. People should be assured of anonymity and encouraged to respond honestly. The format could be simple. For example:

On a scale of 1 to 10, please rate the following:
1. Congregational involvement _____
2. Clarity of worship theme _____
3. Quality of the special music _____
4. Relevance of the sermon _____

The results of this survey should serve as a guide for future changes.

5. *Develop a step-by-step strategy to improve all areas of weakness.* The worship committee should carefully address every issue, designing a step-by-step strategy for change. Consider these questions: What is wrong or missing? How should we add or improve? When will this change begin? Who will be responsible? What resources will be needed? Before any change is implemented, the committee should have a detailed blueprint before it.

6. *The pastor should preach a series of sermons on worship.*

Most congregations are unaware of the biblical instructions on worship. Preaching can instruct and prepare people for the upcoming changes. They will be able to see and understand the biblical roots of these "new" practices. Instead of rejecting these new ideas, people are willing to submit to scriptural guidelines. Pastors must be sure to instruct people in how to be effective worshipers. It should not be assumed people understand such principles and practices simply because they attend church services.

7. *Pastors must proceed slowly.* I cannot overemphasize this point. More than once I stopped change because I pushed too hard too soon. People became threatened as I reshaped everything they knew and valued. Their reaction to my enthusiasm was negative. They would dig in their heels and refuse to move. My evaluation was always, "They are resisting the Spirit." In truth, they were resisting my push for immediate change. Wise pastors take time to implement changes. They begin small, moving to greater issues over time. People, having trusted the pastor on small changes, will soon agree to other, more crucial ones. It is important to identify all red-flag issues. Patience and tender loving care are always the right prescription.

8. *Pastors and worship leaders must move prayerfully toward change.* Mere human effort on spiritual matters is worthless. It may generate activity, but it cannot affect much of eternal importance. True Christian service must be backed with prayer. Pastors and worship leaders desperately need the Spirit's guidance and empowerment. He alone leads us to design truly dynamic worship services. Prayer also is the weapon we use against the enemy. His efforts to thwart change and bring division must be met head-on with prayer. Prayer must be part of every worship committee meeting and a priority of every member.

9. *Pastors must lead their congregations to build for the future.* Most congregations do not have resources on hand for much of what has been discussed. But they should start preparing for the future. Investments should be made in first-class books on worship, good chorus books, audiovisual equipment and puppets for children's sermons. Also, people should be encouraged to attend training seminars on worship—even at church expense. If the topic is not immediately relevant for the church, it can be an investment for the future. Quality worship demands creativity and constant change.

10. *Local churches should hire a full-time minister of worship and music.* Most churches hire their first staff member in youth work, Christian education or as a general associate. I appreciate the importance of each of these areas. I believe, however, that our first and greatest investment should be made in worship. It should be the top priority of the local church. Worship has a tremendous effect on every aspect of Christian life and ministry. It is the source of strength, power and growth. But for many churches, it is the weakest part of their ministry. I am encouraged to see more and more churches hiring full-time staff for worship. When Spirit-filled and creative, these ministers can initiate transforming changes, and churches can come alive with a new vitality and sense of expectation.

Worship is the local church's greatest privilege and most serious responsibility. Pastors and leaders must commit themselves to designing well-balanced and exciting weekly services. These suggestions are but the first steps to that end. While this resource is but a beginning, it can launch churches to new levels of worship and praise. Services can be designed that will accomplish the four main priorities of worship. I pray that churches can move on to experience the height, breadth and depth of worship that glorifies God, focuses on Christ, edifies believers and appeals to visitors. When they do, exciting things are bound to happen!

Worship and Holiness

WOULD GOD EVER TELL HIS PEOPLE to stop worshiping him? It sounds ridiculous, doesn't it? Especially in light of what we've learned about the nature of worship. Yet there have been times when that was precisely the Father's message to a group of His children. It happens when people fail to seek after holiness and righteousness. Training and preparation in worship are to no avail if worshipers compromise in their relationship with God.

Consider these shocking words from God, delivered by the prophet Amos, a spokesman of the Lord Almighty.

> I hate, despise your religious feasts;
> I cannot stand your assemblies.
> Even though you bring me burnt offerings and grain offerings,
> I will not accept them.
> Though you bring choice fellowship offerings,
> I have no regard for them.
> Away with the noise of your songs!
> I will not listen to the music of your harps.
> (Amos 5:21–23)

Every act condemned by God in this oracle had been

previously commended to the people of Israel. They were forms of worship, embraced and accepted for generations. Why did God, who delights in worship, despise and turn His back upon their sacrifices?

Or consider a similar rebuke recorded in the book of Malachi. God, speaking through the prophet, wished that the temple doors were closed to worship and condemned the fires on his altar as useless. He said,

> I am not pleased with you . . . and will accept no offering from your hands. (Malachi 1:10)

Why in these and other cases in Scripture did God take such a stance against worship? The context of each reference gives the answer. While God's people were thoroughly versed in the practices of praise, their lifestyles were characterized by rebellion and wickedness. They were greedy, adulterous, and deceptive. The poor were oppressed, the widowed forgotten, and the weak exploited. Seeing these actions made Sabbath displays of loyalty and love a stench in the nostrils of God.

A well-designed worship service can be an exhilarating experience. In any one hour a person could observe worshipers singing, kneeling, lifting hands and engaging in a dramatic presentation. If properly planned, sights and sounds could be coordinated to communicate a positive, inspiring message to everyone present. It is possible to experience a worship service at a highly stimulating and emotional level. As a result, dynamic worship can draw quite a crowd of people. Since writing this book in 1988, and consulting with countless pastors, I have seen this very thing happen. Churches, previously plateaued or declining, experienced new growth as changes were made to strengthen worship.

That is why I feel called of God to sound a warning. The actions of worship are symbolic, each in its own powerful way, of a loving and faithful relationship between God and his people. They are meant to be outward expressions of deep intimacy between a holy God and His blood-bought people. For individuals to be schooled in the practices of worship as a means of spiritual exhilaration is wrong. Worship should never be adulterated in such an ungodly, self-serving way.

The relationship of husband and wife is often employed within Scripture to symbolize the intimacy and faithfulness God wants to have with His people. Using this metaphor, let me illustrate the issue at hand. Imagine, if you will, a husband who demonstrates love and faithfulness to his wife. He is generous, protective, and affirming. He demonstrates deep affection through every possible means. His commitment is unquestionable and his devotion constant and clearly displayed.

Now, continuing with the metaphor, imagine a wife who in turn is unfaithful in virtually every way. She ignores her husband, spending long periods of time apart from him. With friends she is flirtatious and complimentary, while abusive and unaffectionate with her spouse. In point of fact, this wife maintains no part of the covenant of marriage—except one. She finds sex, the deepest and in some ways most exhilarating act of intimacy, both exciting and desirable. And so, this one "privilege" she offers her husband, though for totally selfish reasons.

How horrible! What a distortion, even perversion of the marriage bond. Certainly you would agree that the exhilarating and fulfilling act of sexual intimacy is meant to be built upon commitment, devotion, and faithfulness between two people. It is an act that symbolizes a day-to-day,

moment-by-moment covenant of love. To expect fulfill-
ment in the act apart from a relationship of mutuality and
permanence is wrong!

It is in this illustration that we find the answer to the
question, "Why does God at times rebuke a congregation
for its worship?" He will not tolerate a people drawn to the
exhilaration of worship, yet walking in open rebellion and
unfaithfulness. The act of worship, as exciting and fulfilling
as it may be, is symbolic of a deep relationship between God
and his people. In that union, God is gracious, pouring
mercy and blessing upon his people. In turn, Christians
respond to God's selfless giving, empowered by the Holy
Spirit to pursue righteousness and holiness.

Put more simply, people engaged in worship on Sunday
must be pursuing righteousness and holiness throughout the
week. They do not do this to earn special favors with God,
since these come by the work of Christ, pure and simply.
The life of obedience, for which Christians are equipped by
the Holy Spirit, is the fruit of a genuine love for the
Redeeming Father. It is this devotion that the believer is to
bring to the celebration of corporate worship.

Practically, pastors are obligated to instruct worshipers in
the biblical requirements of God's covenant relationship.
This entire issue hit me quite powerfully through the in-
credible growth of Risen King Community Church. As has
already been mentioned, RKCC grew from a handful of
people to over 800 in two years. Foundational to this
dramatic growth was a commitment to dynamic worship.
The services were exciting and as a result people came. Week
after week I watched with amazement as new faces joined
our fast-growing family. Regularly newcomers commented
on the power of the worship service, assuring us that they
would return. And, because of our commitment to instruc-

tion, it would not be long before they too were engaging in the acts of worship.

At first, I had nothing but positive feelings about our growth. But one day, while waiting before the Lord, the Holy Spirit led me through the passages mentioned at the beginning of this chapter. Quite frankly, I was gripped by a sudden fear. Could it be that we were guilty of this same unfaithfulness that disqualified the Israelites?

Immediately, I set a course to address this issue with our people. Instruction included sermons on our covenant relationship, repentance, holiness, and our identity in Christ. Following this, we began a church-wide foundational study through First and Second Corinthians. In addition, our leaders reaffirmed growth groups as vital to spiritual growth and maturity, providing a context for vulnerability and accountability.

Five years ago, when I began writing *Exalt Him!* I was deeply passionate about the principles addressed in this volume. Today, I still believe they can serve to bring new life to corporate worship celebrations. But, with humble honesty I confess that the work was incomplete. It needed the material contained in this Epilogue. I pray that pastors and worship leaders heed the warning! It is not enough to teach people to fully engage in the exhilarating acts of worship. We *must* instruct worshipers to live faithful to the covenant relationship we symbolize during corporate worship.

Worship Guide:
Pascack Bible Church

Restoration of Biblical Worship

Just what kind of a church is Pascack Bible Church? Our desire is to be known as a church that takes the Bible seriously and flows with God's Spirit out of the richness of the historic evangelical faith.

We want to be in step with God's Spirit today, never being content to rest upon yesterday's word or work. God has a new word for us today and a new work. We are committed to challenge our most comfortable traditions even at the risk of our own discomfort.

We want PBC to be a loving fellowship of people where you can grow too. We are growing constantly and, therefore, find we are changing—for the better, we hope!

We do things a little differently at PBC. Our worship services deliberately encourage a great deal of congregational involvement. In other words, worship is not a "spectator sport" at PBC. We desire to come into line with the biblical guidelines for corporate worship.

You may see some things in our worship and fellowship with which you are unfamiliar or initially uncomfortable. Many of us began where you are, so we can appreciate how you might feel. You may ask,

Why do you use all kinds of instruments in worship?

> Praise him with the sounding of the trumpet,
>   praise him with the harp and lyre,
> praise him with tambourine and dancing,
>   praise him with the strings and flute,
> praise him with the clash of cymbals,
>   praise him with resounding cymbals.
>   (Psalm 150:3–5)

> And the priests praised the Lord day after day with loud instruments to the LORD. (2 Chronicles 30:21)

Why do some of you raise your hands?

> I will praise you as long as I live,
>   and in your name I will lift up my hands. (Psalm 63:4)

> Lift up your hands in the sanctuary
>   and praise the LORD. (134:2)

> I want men everywhere to lift up holy hands in prayer, without anger or disputing. (1 Timothy 2:8)

Why do some of you audibly, and occasionally loudly, praise the Lord?

> Sing to him a new song;
>   play skillfully, and shout for joy. (Psalm 33:3)

> I will extol the LORD at all times;
>   his praise will always be on my lips. (34:1)

. . . stood up to praise the LORD, the God of Israel, with very loud voice. (2 Chronicles 20:19)

Why do some of you clap your hands?

Clap your hands, all you nations;
  shout to God with cries of joy. (Psalm 47:1)

Why are there sometimes periods of absolute silence?

Occasionally we will sense the presence of the Lord like Isaiah the prophet did (Isaiah 6:1), and our only response can be silence.

The LORD is in his holy temple;
  let all the earth be silent before him. (Habakkuk 2:20)

Why does the congregation sometimes kneel in worship?

In sensing His presence, we want to express a humble acceptance of His Lordship over our lives and corporate worship.

Come, let us bow down in worship,
  let us kneel before the LORD our Maker . . .
    (Psalm 95:6)

Why do we sing new songs as well as hymns?

Sing to him a new song . . . (33:3)

Let the word of Christ dwell in you richly as you teach and admonish one another . . . as you sing psalms, hymns and spiritual songs with gratitude in your hearts to God. (Colossians 3:16)

Why does someone occasionally speak as though he or she were speaking directly from the Lord?

This is called *prophecy* and is meant to rebuke, challenge or encourage God's people in a specific way. (The Elders [spiritual leaders] of the church are responsible to spiritually evaluate what is spoken and then confirm the message or rebuke the speaker in a loving and orderly manner.)

Everyone who prophesies speaks to men for their strengthening, encouragement and comfort. . . . he who prophesies edifies the church. (1 Corinthians 14:3–4)

Two or three prophets should speak [at the most], and the others should weigh carefully what is said. . . . Everything should be done in a fitting and orderly way. (14:29, 40)

Why do you often invite people to the front for prayer at the close of the service?

Our greatest joy is to be able to further explain God's way of salvation to anyone in the congregation who has questions and wants to know how to accept Jesus Christ as Savior. But there are other reasons for people to come forward to the altar:

For healing and forgiveness—"Confess your sins to each other and pray for each other so that you may be healed. . . . My brothers, if one of you should wander from the truth and someone should bring him back, remember this: Whoever turns a sinner from the error of his way will save him from death and cover over a multitude of sins." (James 5:16, 19–20)

For encouragement—"And let us consider how we may spur one another on toward love and good deeds. Let us not give up meeting together, as some are in the habit of doing, but let us encourage one another." (Hebrews 10:24–25)

To allow people to publicly confess Jesus Christ as their Lord—"That if you confess with your mouth, 'Jesus is Lord,' and believe in your heart that God raised him from the dead, you will be saved. For it is with your heart that you believe and are justified, and with your mouth that you confess and are saved." (Romans 10:9–10)

Why do the elders anoint with oil and pray for the sick when they are called upon to do so?

Is anyone of you sick [serious illness]? He should call the elders of the church to pray over him and anoint him with oil in the name of the Lord. And the prayer offered in faith will make the sick person well; the Lord will raise him up. If he has sinned, he will be forgiven. (James 5:14–15)

Here's an explanation of some terminology that might be new to you.

Church—Not the building, but the people of God "called out of the world" to manifest an allegiance to

Jesus Christ above all other authorities.

Body—Another name for the church, the "body" of believers who are a new expression of the very life of Jesus Himself, who is called the "head" of that body.

Amen—A word that has been used by people for centuries as an endorsement of that which acknowledges our God.

Hallelujah—Literally it means, "praise Yahweh." Yahweh is the name for God. An enthusiastic and joyful endorsement of our God and His works.

Praise—The act of drawing attention to the person and works of God, including the rehearsal of His very nature.

Glory—The manifestation of God's presence and splendor to man's spiritual and physical senses.

Worship—The act of ascribing worth to God by all who gather in His name. It is an act done personally that is woven together with others in corporate expressions like singing, praising, endorsing God's Word with "Amens," even offering oneself in acts of sacrificial service.

Minister—Serving or helping others in the name of Jesus and under the power of Jesus.

Used by permission of Dr. Fred Beveridge
Pascack Bible Church
181 Piermont Avenue, Hillsdale, New Jersey 07692

An Alternate Order of Worship

Prelude
Announcements
Silent Preparation

Songs of Gathering: calling God's people together to approach the throne of God.

Greetings/Extending Peace

Call to Worship: Scripture or song

Songs of Praise/Adoration: moving worshipers toward the inner court; give opportunity for confession/forgiveness.

Phrases of Praise
Testimony

Ministry of the Word:
  Prayers
  Scripture
  Drama
  Sermon
  Response

Songs of Thanksgiving

Offering
Doxology

Ministry of healing: prayers for the burdened and ill, including the anointing of oil/laying on of hands.

Songs of Rejoicing

Benediction

Worship Planning Sheet

Date:
Sermon theme:
Sermon purpose:
Sermon title:
Sermon text:

Worship checklist (elements to be used in this service):

____prelude	____children's sermon
____call to worship	____Scripture
____hymns	____benediction
____choruses	____testimony
____creed	____puppets
____responsive reading	____choir anthem
____silent meditation	____special music
____drama	____communion
____greeting of visitors	____baptism/dedication
____missionary moment	____reception of members
____Lord's Prayer	____sermon
____pastoral prayer	____confession
____offering	____announcements
____offertory	____ministry of healing
____doxology	____open praise/prayer
____Gloria Patri	____other_____

Hymns:

1. _____

2. _____

3. _____

Choruses:

1. _____

2. _____

3. _____

Special Music:

1. _____

2. _____

Responsive reading, p. _____

Scripture reading _____

Order of service:

Announcements: _____

_____

Prelude

_____

_____

_____

_____

_____

Benediction: _____

Postlude

_____

_____

_____

Philosophy checklist:

Will this service glorify God?

  Sacrificial?   Sincere?

  Sensible?   Spirit-filled?

Is this service Christ-centered?
  Retell?   Remember?
  Rejoice?   Respond?

Will this service edify believers?
  Inspire?   Instruct?
  Involve?   Integrate?

Will this service appeal to visitors?
  Comfortable?   Clear?
  Convincing?   Creative?

Notes: (Use to write down any specific instructions for ushers, worship team, musicians, greeters, communion stewards, sound person, lighting coordinator, etc.)

Worship

Abba, Raymond. *Principles of Christian Worship*. New York: Oxford University Press, 1960.

Abernathy, William B. *New Look for Sunday Morning*. Nashville: Abingdon Press, 1975.

Allen, Ronald and Gordon Borror. *Worship, Rediscovering the Missing Jewel*. Portland, OR: Multnomah Press, 1982.

Allen, Ronald Barclay. *Praise! A Matter of Life and Breath*. Nashville: Thomas Nelson Publishers, 1980.

Bailey, Robert W. *New Ways in Christian Worship*. Nashville: Broadman Press, 1981.

Bailey, Wilfred M. *Awakened Worship*. Nashville: Abingdon Press, 1972.

Burkhart, John E. *Worship*. Philadelphia: Westminster Press, 1982.

Coffin, Henry S. *The Public Worship of God*. Philadelphia: Westminster, 1946.

Cullman, Oscar. *Early Christian Worship*. Naperville, IL: Allenson, 1953.

Erickson, Craig Douglas. *Participating in Worship*. Louisville, KY: Westminister/John Knox Press, 1989.

Garrett, Thomas S. *Christian Worship, an Introductory Outline*. New York: Oxford, 1973.

Hardin, Grady. *The Leadership of Worship*. Nashville: Abingdon Press, 1980.

Hickman, Hoyt L. *A Primer for Church Worship.* Nashville: Abingdon Press, 1984.

Hinnebusch, Paul O.P. *Praise: A Way of Life.* Ann Arbor: Servant Books, 1976.

Hoon, Paul W. *The Integrity of Worship.* Nashville: Abingdon Press, 1971.

Jennings, Theodore W. *Life as Worship.* Grand Rapids: William B. Eerdmans Publishing Co., 1982.

Liesch, Barry. *People in the Presence of God.* Grand Rapids: Zondervan, 1988.

Martin, Ralph P. *Worship in the Early Church.* London: Marshall, Morgan & Scott, 1964.

_____. *The Worship of God.* Grand Rapids: William B. Eerdmans Publishing Co., 1982.

Miller, Calvin. *The Table of Inwardness.* Downers Grove, IL: InterVarsity Press, 1984.

Morey, Robert A. *Worship Is All of Life.* Camp Hill, PA: Christian Publications, 1984.

Ortlund, Anne. *Up With Worship.* Glendale, CA: Gospel Light Publications, 1975.

Prime, Derek. *Created to Praise.* Downers Grove, IL : Inter-Varsity Press, 1981.

Rayburn, Robert G. *O Come Let Us Worship.* Grand Rapids: Baker Book House, 1980.

Schaper, Robert N. *In His Presence.* Nashville: Thomas Nelson Publishers, 1984.

Tozer, A.W. *Whatever Happened to Worship?* Camp Hill, PA: Christian Publications, 1985.

_____. *Worship, The Missing Jewel of the Evangelical Church.* Camp Hill, PA: Christian Publications, n.d.

Underhill, Evelyn. *Worship.* New York: Harper & Row, n.d.

Wagner, C. Peter. *What Are We Missing?* Altamonte Springs, FL: Creation House, 1972.

Webber, Robert E. *Worship Is a Verb.* Waco, TX: Word Books, 1985.

_____. *Worship: Old and New.* Grand Rapids: Zondervan 1982.

White, James F. *Christian Worship in Transition.* Nashville: Abingdon Press, 1976.

_____. *Introduction to Christian Worship.* Nashville: Abingdon Press, 1980.

_____. *New Forms of Worship.* Nashville: Abingdon Press, 1971.

Willimon, William H. and Robert L. Wilson, *Preaching and Worship in the Small Church.* Nashville: Abingdon Press, 1980.

_____. *Word, Water, Wine and Bread: How Worship Has Changed Over the Years.* Valley Forge, PA: Judson Press, 1980.

Sermon Construction and Delivery

Adams, Jay E. *Preaching with Purpose.* Grand Rapids: Baker Book House, 1982.

Baumann, J. Daniel. *An Introduction to Contemporary Preaching.* Grand Rapids: Baker Book House, 1972.

Broadus, John A. *On the Preparation and Delivery of Sermons.* Nashville: Broadman Press, 1986.

Buechner, F. Frederick. *Telling the Truth: The Gospel as Tragedy, Comedy and Fairy Tale.* New York: Harper & Row, 1977.

Cox, James W. *A Guide to Biblical Preaching.* Nashville: Abingdon Press, 1976.

Craddock, Fred. *Preaching*. Nashville: Abingdon Press, 1985.

Davis, Henry G. *Design for Preaching*. Philadelphia: Fortress Press, 1958.

Kaiser, Walter C. *Toward an Exegetical Theology*. Grand Rapids: Baker Book House, 1981.

Killinger, John. *Fundamentals of Preaching*. Philadelphia: Fortress Press, 1985.

Lloyd-Jones, D. Martyn. *Joy Unspeakable*. Wheaton, IL: Harold Shaw Publishers, 1984

_____. *Preaching and Preachers*. Grand Rapids: Zondervan, 1974.

Markquart, Edward F. *Quest for Better Preaching*. Minnesota: Augsburg, 1985.

Perry, Lloyd M. *Biblical Preaching for Today's World*. Chicago: Moody Press, 1973.

_____. and Charles M. Sell, *Speaking to Life's Problems*. Chicago: Moody Press, n.d.

Pitt-Watson, Ian. *Preaching: A Kind of Folly*. Philadelphia: Westminster Press, 1976.

_____. *A Primer for Preachers*. Grand Rapids: Baker Book House, 1987.

Robinson, Haddon W. *Biblical Preaching*. Grand Rapids: Baker Book House, 1980.

Stott, John R.W. *Between Two Worlds*. Grand Rapids: William B. Eerdmans Publishing Co., 1982.

NOTES

1. Robert G. Rayburn, *O Come Let Us Worship. Corporate Worship in the Evangelical Church* (Grand Rapids: Baker Book House, 1980), p. 11.

2. A.W. Tozer, *The Pursuit of God* (Camp Hill, PA: Christian Publications, 1982), p. 38.

3. R.B. Allen, *Praise! A Matter of Life and Breath* (Nashville: Broadman Press, 1980), p. 9.

4. This diagram is a modification of one suggested by Dr. John Kenneth Smith, pastor of Otterbein United Methodist Church, Connellsville, Pennsylvania.

5. Robert Webber, *Worship Old and New* (Grand Rapids: Zondervan Publishing House, 1982), pp. 11–12.

6. Ralph Martin, *Worship in the Early Church* (Grand Rapids: William B. Eerdmans Publishing Company, 1974), p. 10.

7. R. Allen and G. Borror, *Worship: Rediscovering the Missing Jewel* (Portland, OR: Multnomah Press, 1982), p. 18.

8. Derek Prime, *Created to Praise* (Downers Grove, IL: InterVarsity Press, 1981), pp. 10–11.

9. Prime, p. 11.

10. Paul Hinnebusch, *Praise: A Way of Life* (Ann Arbor: Servant Books, 1976), p. 4.

11. William Temple, *Readings in St. John's Gospel* (MacMillan, 1942), p. 68.

12. R. Allen and G. Borror, p. 23.

13. David C. Cook Publishers developed a delightful

video featuring David and Karen Mains. In it, they discuss preparation for worship. Their insights are valuable and would greatly help leaders instruct their people in ways to prepare for Sunday morning. The title of this series is *What Makes the Christian Family Christian?* Order from Christian Publications, Camp Hill, PA 17011.

14. D. Martyn Lloyd-Jones, *Joy Unspeakable* (Wheaton, IL: Harold Shaw Publishers, 1984), p. 16.

15. A. Campolo, *How to be Pentecostal without Speaking in Tongues* (Waco, TX: Word Books, 1991), p. 2.

16. Robert Webber, *Worship Is a Verb* (Waco, TX: Word Books, 1985), p. 4.

17. James W. Cox, *A Guide to Biblical Preaching*, (Nashville: Abingdon Press, 1976), p. 45–46).

18. Ian Pitt-Watson, *A Primer for Preachers* (Grand Rapids: Baker Book House, 1986), p. 10.

19. Pitt-Watson, p. 17

20. John R.W. Stott, *Between Two Worlds* (Grand Rapids: William B. Eerdmans Publishing Company, 1982), p. 226.

21. Stott, p. 226.

22. Edward F. Marquart, *Quest for Better Preaching*, (Minneapolis: Augsburg Press, 1985), p. 152.

23. Jay Adams, *Preaching with Purpose* (Grand Rapids: Baker Book House, 1982), p. 1.

24. Adams, p. 31.

25. Daniel J. Baumann, *Introduction to Contemporary Preaching* (Grand Rapids: Baker Book House, 1972), p. 243.

26. C. Peter Wagner, *What Are We Missing?* (Altamonte Springs, FL: Creation House, 1972), p. 110–111.

27. Terry Wardle, "Training Worshippers: A Key to Effective Worship," *The Pastors Update* Vol. 2 No. 12. Sept. 1991.

28. Stott, p. 138–139.

29. Michael Green, *I Believe in the Holy Spirit* (Grand Rapids: William B. Eerdmans Publishing Co., 1975), p. 113.

30. D. Martyn Lloyd-Jones, *Joy Unspeakable*, p. 102.

31. Doug Murren, *The Baby Boomerang* (Ventura, CA: Regal Books, 1990), p. 217.